High Fibre
HIGH FLAVOUR

High Fibre
HIGH FLAVOUR

More than 180 delicious recipes for good health

ROSEMARY MOON

David & Charles

A David & Charles Book

First Published in the UK in 2000 by David & Charles

Copyright © 2000 Quintet Publishing Limited
6 Blundell Street
London N7 9BH

A catalogue record for this book is available from the British Library

ISBN 0-7153-1118-2

FBPR

This book was conceived, designed, and produced by
Quintet Publishing Limited
6 Blundell Street
London N7 9BH

for David & Charles
Brunel House
Newton Abbot
Devon

Project Editor: Laura Price
Art Director: Simon Daley
Editor: Anna Bennett
Designer: Paul Wright
Photographers: Ian Garlick and Andrew Sydenham
Food Stylists: Kathryn Hawkins and Rosemary Moon

Creative Director: Richard Dewing
Publisher: Oliver Salzmann

Typeset in Great Britain by
Central Southern Typesetters, Eastbourne
Manufactured in Hong Kong by Regent Publishing Services Ltd.
Printed in Singapore by Star Standard Industries Pte. Ltd.

Contents

Introduction

Eating is one of the greatest pleasures in life for many of us privileged to live in relative security and affluence in the Western world. There is so much available to us; virtually every fruit and vegetable can be found fresh throughout the year on supermarket shelves, and almost all the ingredients for any style of national or international cuisine can be found without difficulty.

Life is made very easy for us. The drudgery and tedium have been removed from so many day-to-day jobs, allowing us more time to live life in the fast lane, to work full-time as well as run a home, to pursue hobbies, sports and other leisure interests throughout the week and not just weekends. Everything is self-cleaning to allow us more time

and foods are being processed and prepared so that we simply have to heat them up.

It is the preparation of food for an easy life that particularly concerns me. Prepared and processed foods cut down dramatically on the time required to produce a meal but it is the things that are added to these foods, like additives and preservatives, and, more importantly, the things that are taken away, like bran and other forms of fibre, that should be carefully considered in terms of a balanced and healthy diet.

Not all processed food products are complete foods or convenience meals; white flour, which has had all the bran removed from it, is a

processed food and so is white rice, which has been polished to remove the outer husk, making it quicker to cook and easier to digest. White flour and refined sugar are good for baking, but the finished cake or bread has little nutritional value, except that it is high in fat and carbohydrates in the form of sugars and starch.

WHAT IS FIBRE?

Fibre has become a buzzword of the modern age, prompted by growing concern about and awareness of a healthy diet. There is a certain amount of irony in this, however, as fibre used to be abundant in our diets and it is only through progress in food production and preparation, and affluence that we have started to remove it from our everyday foods. Now, we are beginning to suffer the consequences.

Dietary fibre is the substance that forms the cell walls of all plants – the superstructure or skeleton of the plant world. There is no dietary fibre in fish, meat or dairy products; it is unique to plants and, as recently as the 1960s, was generally disregarded as being of no nutritional value. The milling and processing of foods was therefore a reasonable idea – getting rid of the tough outer coating to reveal a more attractive and easily digestible food.

Every age has common diseases and every set of circumstances poses problems regarding health. So many of the diseases that are now common in the Western world were far less prevalent in the past, and there is an obvious link between many intestinal disorders and the processed, soggy diet of our busy, affluent society. In the less developed countries of the world – where the staple diet of many is rice, lentils and vegetables – there is also disease, but in many cases it is associated with vitamin deficiencies rather than with a lack of dietary fibre.

There is now significant evidence that a healthy diet – one rich in fibre – can help to prevent many of the so-called "modern diseases" that are especially linked with the digestive system, such as diabetes, gallstones, appendicitis, and disorders of the bowel, as well as heart disease. To keep as healthy an internal system as possible, it is important to cook with and eat as many unprocessed foods as possible. This leads us inevitably towards a high-fibre diet.

THE BASIC PRINCIPLES OF A HIGH-FIBRE DIET

Eating a high-fibre diet is little more than common sense, a "back-to-nature" approach to eating. This means using fresh foods whenever possible, or frozen foods such as vegetables and prawns. It also means using basic products that have been processed as little as possible to maintain their fibre content.

The most obvious example of this is the milling of wheat and the production of flour. Once milling was an established mechanical process rather than being carried out by hand in small quantities between two stones, it became fashionable to eat white bread. This is made from flour that not only has been milled, but has had all the bran (the outer fibrous husk) sieved out of it. White bread was, and by many people still is, considered to be light, attractive in colour, and soft to eat. Eventually, commercial steam bakeries were introduced, producing a moist, spongy white bread to be sliced and packed in plastic bags before sale. It seems to me that every last trace of fibre has been removed from such bread, as well as the ability to satisfy the appetite. Sure enough, for the devoted white bread eater, there are now commercial loaves with grains added to provide some dietary fibre, following the realization that fibre-rich foods are essential to a healthy modern diet; but a loaf made with whole-wheat flour must surely make a better choice of bread than that.

EATING FOR PLEASURE AND FOR HEALTH

I find the word "diet" can be off-putting. Eating is, for me, a great pleasure, the taste, texture and combination of foods in any dish being the secret of a delicious meal. "Diet", with its connotations of weight reduction or a strict health regime, implies deprivation. Eating healthily does not mean having to endure dull or unappetizing food. On the contrary, including fibre-rich foods in a healthy, modern diet is far more pleasurable than it sounds!

The secret of success when changing from one eating habit to another is to enjoy the challenge and to be motivated. A high-fibre way of life requires you to eat plenty of fruit and vegetables, less meat and dairy products and more natural cereals, grains and legumes. It is a regime that makes sense to anyone interested in health and the environment and, more importantly, to anyone interested in food and cooking.

AN INTRODUCTION TO HIGH-FIBRE FOODS

There is a tendency to associate high-fibre foods almost exclusively with vegetarian cookery. This is an easy mistake, as the high-fibre diet is based on grains, cereals, beans and pulses, all of which are vegetarian foods. These foods also serve to cut down on the amount of animal proteins that non-vegetarians eat and to provide more variety in our food.

It is important that we try to reduce the amount of meat and dairy products we consume, and combining these foods with others high in fibre provides a sensible and balanced diet.

Fresh fruit and vegetables contain significant amounts of fibre and should certainly be included in all eating regimes, not only for their fibre but also for their valuable vitamins and minerals. As a matter of taste (which is, after all, what eating is about for those of us who are not simply eating to

survive), many of us prefer our vegetables cooked, especially root vegetables such as potatoes and turnips, to make them more pleasant and more easily digestible. It is, however, a good idea to try to eat some raw foods every day – if you eat four different kinds of raw fruit, you will be doing well. Some vegetables, such as carrots and celery, make quick and easy snacks as an alternative to fruit. It is also good to get into the habit of eating a fresh salad every day.

TO PEEL OR NOT TO PEEL

To gain the maximum amount of dietary fibre from fruit and vegetables, you should eat them unpeeled. This is naturally a matter of taste, but it can also depend on where you buy your

vegetables and how they are grown. Modern farming methods have become extremely reliant on pesticides, which often leave residues on the produce or in the soil. For the wonderful flavour of young carrots, freshly dug, washed and steamed, go for organically grown produce.

In most of the recipes in this book, I have not specified whether vegetables and fruit should be peeled or not – that is a matter of individual preference. By all means peel carrots for carrot cake, but leave them whole for casseroles, risottos and salads. If you do peel your vegetables, however, put the peelings to good use – they make an excellent flavouring for vegetable stock, but remember to strain the peelings from the stock before use.

Cereals and grains

These may sound like two completely separate groups of foods but they are really just one and the same. Grain is the fruit or seed of a cereal and it is a term frequently applied to wheat and other food-related grasses and their fruit or seeds. A cereal may be defined as being of wheat or another edible grain, and is also the name applied to foods that are made from grains, for example, breakfast cereals.

THE HISTORY OF GRAINS

Grains, the basic foodstuff of the world, really changed the face of civilization once humans set about cultivating them.

Early humans were nomadic and opportunistic eaters, hunting and adding wild fruit, berries and plants to the basic diet. They travelled around, especially to look for grazing once they started to domesticate animals. Ancient forms of wheat and other grains grew in the wild and it was found that the seeds from these could be eaten. They became more palatable if the outer husks were removed and the grains ground between stones and mixed to a paste for baking. They also kept well, especially if picked when fully ripe and dry, and could therefore be stored.

It may well have been a chance discovery – a lucky accident that changed the life of early humans – when it was found that these grains, scattered over the land, would grow again, yielding another crop for another year. However, once humans made a conscious decision to grow grains, rather than just harvesting them when found by chance, it became necessary to stay in one place in order to nurture the crop and harvest it. So humans decided to abandon the nomadic life and, literally, put down roots.

BASIC CROPS THROUGHOUT THE WORLD

Wheat and barley are known to have been the earliest crops and were grown throughout the early world in the Middle East. As humans travelled out across the continents, they took their early crops with them, and these grains became staple foods for early Chinese, Egyptian and Indian peoples. All crops have their ideal growing conditions, and it became clear that, while these crops thrived in hot and sunny climates, they did not fare well in very wet areas. Other grains, however, such as oats, rye and buckwheat, were successful and humans began to incorporate these in crops. It is thought that at first these crops may well have grown as weeds among wheat and barley, struggling in the warmer Mediterranean climate, but were eventually found to flourish in colder and wetter conditions.

Millet, a cereal that is not as common in Western cooking as in other cuisines, is extremely tolerant of high temperatures and grows well in Africa and Asia, where it can withstand very hot and dry, almost arid, conditions. Another grain that can withstand heat but must have plenty of moisture is rice, which is grown, half-submerged in water, in the paddy fields of China, India and Southeast Asia. Rice is also grown in Italy, Spain and North America, but in much smaller quantities. The countries that produce the majority of the world's rice are some of the most densely populated areas of the world, and rice remains the staple food of more than half the world's population.

ABOVE LEEK AND SPINACH BARLEY SOUP (SEE PAGE 56)

Maize, or corn, was one of the oldest crops in the Americas, but the original wild crop is thought to have died out many thousands of years ago. It must have been able to regenerate by self-sowing in the wild, but the modern corn kernel remains firmly and tightly attached to the cob, its natural carrier. Modern corn would not continue if it were not harvested from the cob and subsequently planted, by hand or machine. Although maize is most commonly found in Africa and the Americas, its indigenous home, it is now grown in some parts of Mediterranean Europe, especially in Italy and Spain, and also in China and India.

GRAINS AND CEREALS

Grains and cereals are the most important source of carbohydrates in the diet, but the amount of fibre yielded by them depends on the extent to which they have been processed. There are three parts to a grain: the outer husk, which is commonly known as the bran and contains most of the fibre; the endosperm, the largest part of the grain which contains most of the starch; and the germ, which contains the kernel or new growth of the plant, and therefore is the grain's source of protein. To benefit from the whole nutritional value of a cereal it is, therefore, essential to eat the whole grain. Milling not

BROWN RICE   WILD RICE   WHEAT

only removes the bran, it also takes away nutrients such as vitamins B and E. Most cereals contain only around 1.5 percent fibre, but compared to other foods we regard them as high-fibre; this shows just how important it is to include them as whole grains in our diet.

Buy all grains and cereals in as natural, or unrefined, a form as possible. It is in the processing of grains that fibre may be lost, so it is important to know what to look for when buying potentially fibre-rich foods. For a high-fibre diet, you should always buy wholewheat flour; this means that it is the whole of the edible grain, with all the bran – the fibre-rich part of the food.

STORING CEREALS AND GRAINS

As these are dry foods, they must be kept dry, either in storage canisters, jars or tubs. Keep all dry goods on shelves rather than on the floor and use them in strict rotation, using the oldest first to avoid keeping very old stock. Even flour does not keep forever, and I find that wholewheat flour is more inclined to become slightly rancid than white flour. Stone-ground flour does not keep as well as ordinary wholewheat flour, although I think it has a finer texture and flavour. Even if you are a very keen baker and make all your own bread, you should not be tempted to buy flour in bulk quantities –

the fresher the better, so use it up quickly. I recommend keeping wholewheat flour for no longer than six months.

COMMON VARIETIES OF CEREALS AND GRAINS

Wheat is still probably the most widely grown grain. The USA, Canada and Russia are the major producers, although it is also grown throughout Western Europe. China, India, Argentina, Australia and Pakistan are other wheat-growing areas. More than ninety percent of wheat is grown in the Northern Hemisphere. Wheat is either hard or soft, the soft being used for general-purpose flours, containing less gluten and protein than the hard. Hard wheat is better for bread flours and for the production of pasta.

Wheat has always been the main crop for the production of **flour** for breadmaking. It contains more gluten – the substance which creates the framework of bread and makes the dough elastic – than other flours and consequently produces a lighter, more palatable loaf. Wholewheat flour, as the name suggests, is milled from the whole grain so contains all the nutrients.

Bulgur is a form of cracked wheat made by boiling and then baking whole grains of wheat, which are then cracked. This technique was probably developed as a method of storage, and bulgur is particularly common in the Middle East. It is most often used in salads such as

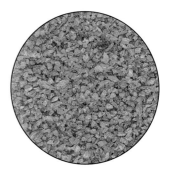

CRACKED WHEAT   MUESLI   BULGUR

tabbouleh, but I also like cooking with it – it makes excellent risotto-style dishes and cooks in approximately the same time as rice.

Wheat flakes are used mainly as a breakfast cereal. **Wheat germ** is the heart of the grain and is generally added to breakfast cereals as a highly nutritious dietary supplement. **Wheat bran** is the most common form of bran and is the by-product of milling white flour. It is rich in fibre and is added to breads or sold to be added to cereals to boost fibre in them.

Semolina and **couscous** are both wheat products. Semolina is a meal ground from durum wheat, a particularly hard form of wheat used in pasta-making. Semolina is used in milk puddings and readily absorbs liquid. I scatter it lightly under fish or meat that is to be cooked wrapped in pastry – the semolina absorbs any juices and prevents the pastry from becoming soggy during cooking. Couscous, pellets of processed fine and coarse semolinas mixed together then sifted into shape, gives its name to a dish when it is steamed over a stew with which it is served.

Barley is available as a whole grain, which is known as **pot barley**, to be used in stews. It may take up to three hours to cook and never really becomes soft and tender. **Pearl barley** is the husked, polished berry and is traditionally used in soups, both for flavour and as a thickener.

Barley flour is used in many eastern European countries to make bread, but it gives a rather grey loaf with a dense texture, and is considerably less palatable than a wheat loaf. It has a sweet flavour, however, and is a useful ingredient in a mixed-grain loaf when combined with wheat and rye flours. Barley may also be used to make a form of oatmeal, but is most commonly associated with the brewing industry, where it is used in the production of malt for both beers and whisky.

Rye is widely grown and used in northern European and Scandinavian countries, being tolerant of cold weather and acid soils. Until the nineteenth century, **rye flour** was more commonly used in some areas for bread than wheat, but as soon as white bread became fashionable, so did wheat flour. Rye flour is used to make "black" breads and crackers. It does not have the same gluten content as wheat so the resulting yeasted breads are heavier and do not rise as much. **Crackers** were originally made to prolong the storage life of the rye crop. Short summers in northern Europe meant that the rye often had to be harvested before it was really ripe, and the unripe grain did not store well, being too full of moisture. Roughly ground and baked into slabs, it was found that these fibre-rich crackers kept well and could be stored right through the long winter months. Some rye is

ABOVE CREAMED CORN CORNBREAD (SEE PAGE 194)

grown in North America and it is often fermented to make rye whiskey. Rye is darker in colour than wheat and has a stronger flavour, although it is sometimes processed into a white flour which then loses most of the distinctive rye flavour.

Somehow **oats** have a far more rustic image than the other grains and cereal crops. They are a hardy crop, and are often made into a gruel or mush. Oats are a soft grain and are therefore not suitable for milling into flour. The crop is adaptable and is thought to have been grown in ancient Mesopotamia and Abyssinia, both of which had very warm climates. It would have provided useful cover for more tender plants, shielding them from the sun. Oats are now

usually grown in colder climates in the Northern Hemisphere, in the USA and Canada, Europe and Russia.

Oats are a good source of iron, potassium and vitamin B, as well as being rich in fibre and carbohydrates, with some protein and fat. **Oat flakes**, or **rolled oats**, are used for baking and for oatmeal, a warming breakfast dish (especially good with brown sugar on very cold days!) **Oatmeal** or **Irish oatmeal** is milled in various grades and may be used for baking, especially oatcakes, and features in the Scottish national dish, haggis. **Oat bran** is the fibre-rich outer casing of the oats. It can be added to most breakfast cereals or mixed with rolled oats for hot oatmeal.

Millet is thought of by many people as little more than bird food, yet it is widely grown and consumed in Africa and in some countries in Asia and Europe. It makes excellent savoury baked goods – it has a creamy texture and must be boiled before being turned into a finished dish – I have used it for rissoles and in baking. It may also be used as a thickener, especially for soups and stews, in which case it should be cooked in the cooking liquid of the dish. It does swell considerably, so don't be tempted to add too much to the dish.

Corn or **maize** is the biggest crop in North America, which grows over forty percent of the world's total production. It grows very high – I have worked in corn fields in southern England where the crop has been taller than I am. The terms corn and maize are interchangeable; therefore, cornflour and maize flour are the same basic product, although they may vary in colour. Corn, when on the cob, is very high in dietary fibre.

Corn is available processed as **cornflour**, a very fine flour used for thickening liquids for sauces, stews and soups. It is generally white. **Cornmeal** and **polenta** are not quite so finely ground and are usually yellow in colour. Polenta is produced in Italy and is generally made into a solid, oatmeal-like substance which is delicious sliced or baked and served with soups or stews. Corn or maize flour is used extensively throughout the USA for bread and gives a much sweeter flavour than wheat flour.

Hominy and **grits** are common foods in the American South. The first is the dried corn kernels, also widely available ready-to-eat in cans. When dry, hominy should be soaked to reconstitute and then baked or fried, although I prefer to use it in casseroles, especially those made with pork. Even when left to soak overnight, hominy may take up to five hours of simmering to soften. Grits are ground hominy and have a semolina-like texture. They cook much more quickly than the whole kernels and are often served with bacon and eggs.

Blue cornmeal is unusual and is highly valued because of its unusual appearance. The flour really is blue and comes from a dark blue strain of corn, which is usually made into tortilla chips or sold for making pancakes. Apart from culinary uses, it may sometimes be found in some cosmetic products, such as face scrubs and deep cleansers.

Popcorn is a particularly hard corn kernel which turns itself inside out when cooked in a popcorn-maker or a dry, covered pan. The pan should be well sealed, otherwise the exploding corn may cover your kitchen. The beneficial fibre content of popcorn is usually more than cancelled out by the amount of butter or salt used to coat it.

One of the more unusual grains available is **buckwheat**, which is really the fruit or seed of a plant closely related to rhubarb and sorrel, and therefore not really a grain at all. It does, however, cook like a grain. It is available both raw and roasted, the latter having a deeper and slightly more palatable flavour. It is rich in vitamins A and B and calcium, as well as carbohydrates. Buckwheat is available as groats (grains) or as flour. The flour, which is an unusual grey colour, is used for pancakes, crêpes and muffins; generally, I find bread made with buckwheat very unappealing and not to my taste. The most common use for buckwheat flour is in the making of pancakes and blinis – little yeasted pancakes most commonly from Russia, which are served with sour cream, caviar and smoked salmon.

Rice is the staple food of about half the population of the world and is grown on every continent except Antarctica. It is a cereal grass and while it is grown on tropical hillsides, it is widely grown in water on marshy flooded land, usually known as paddy-fields, in conditions in which other grains – such as barley and wheat – would not survive.

Rice is native to India and Indo-China but its cultivation quickly spread throughout the East. Ancient Chinese records speak of planting ceremonies after permission to grow rice had been granted by the emperor. The term "paddy-field" actually comes from the Malay word *padi* for unhusked rice grains.

The Romans brought rice back to Italy following their travels to the East and grew it in the flooded plains of the Po Valley. Arborio rice, used to make risotto, is grown there to this day. As the Roman Empire expanded, so too did the cultivation of rice, moving to Spain and parts of Africa. Today, there is also a great deal of rice grown in the USA, but this really came about by accident when a spice ship from Madagascar, bound for England, was blown off course, and ended up in Charleston, South Carolina. In gratitude to his hosts for their hospitality, the captain of the ship presented them with some of his cargo of rough seed rice, which has flourished in the South ever since.

THE NUTRITIVE VALUE OF RICE

Rice is not fattening; like pasta, it's the food you serve with it that can do the damage! All rices are valuable sources of B-group vitamins and minerals, especially potassium and phosphorus. Brown rice contains both more fibre and more protein than white rice and is also a good source of calcium and iron.

Brown rice is simply the unmilled or unpolished grain, so all varieties of rice should be available as brown rice. It is quite easy to find brown long grain, short grain, and basmati rices, and brown arborio rice is sometimes available in good health shops. Brown rice takes longer to cook than white; never add salt to the water during cooking because this can toughen the grain. The cooking time may be slightly shortened by soaking the rice in the measured amount of water before cooking.

Instant or **converted rice** is partially steamed before the milling process. This forces the nutrients from the bran into the rice grain so that they are retained during milling. Instant brown rice is now widely available.

There are many other types of rice, most of which are most commonly available in their white or polished forms. Among my favourites are **arborio** and **carnarolli** rice, both used to make **risotto**, and **basmati**, the finest grain of all the rices, which is grown in the foothills of the Himalayas. **Camargue red rice** is an unpolished rice grown in very small quantities in southern France, which has a very nutty flavour as well as a very distinctive colour.

Wild rice is actually the seed from an aquatic grass grown in the northern USA and in Canada. It has very long, slender, almost-black grains. Originally very expensive, being hand-harvested from a boat, wild rice is now grown commercially, although the cultivated grains do not have quite the same flavour as the truly wild variety. Wild rice has a far higher nutritive value than either of the two main cereal crops, regular rice and wheat. Its protein contains all nine of the

ABOVE WILD RICE QUICK BREAD (SEE PAGE 190)

essential amino acids, making it a complete protein. Because it is unpolished, it is also very rich in fibre.

Rice bran is the husk of the rice, removed during milling. It is not a common product except in countries where rice is processed, but it is used as a supplement to breakfast cereals. **Flaked rice** cooks quickly and is used mainly in puddings,

although it is often added to muesli. **Rice flour** is used especially in Chinese cookery to make rice noodles, but can also be used to thicken sauces and in cakes and pastries for people who are allergic to wheat flour. It is very fine and is often used in the cosmetics industry as a base for makeup. **Ground rice** is the rice equivalent of semolina, fine and grainy and used for puddings and cookies.

Beans: dried foods rich in nutrients

Beans and legumes are not only a good source of fibre in the diet – red kidney beans, for example, contain 4.5 per cent fibre and as much protein as meat (24 per cent), and much the same is true of chickpeas and lentils – all beans also contain vitamins, especially B-group, and minerals, notably iron. There is a wide variety of beans in different shapes and colours, making them an invaluable part of our diet. From the eating angle most of them taste remarkably similar; however, chickpeas and adzuki beans are in my opinion outstanding in their flavour. After that, the choice is governed by appearance, the dish for which they are intended, and the length of cooking time available.

For the recipes in this book, I have used my favourite beans, the ones that I generally have in my cupboard. I have not included any recipes for soya beans, for example, as I do not keep them at home. They could, however, be used in any of the recipes calling for a similar size of bean; for example, haricot beans or black-eyed peas.

Adzuki, or azuki beans are common in Chinese and Japanese cooking and grow in both countries. They are a rich, nutty brown in colour and very small. The most obvious feature of the beans is their slightly sweet flavour – they are often used in sweet dishes – and I have included them in both a savoury casserole and a delicious sweet dessert cobbler.

Mung beans are a similar size to adzuki beans but are green in colour. They may be sprouted for a salad vegetable, and are sometimes ground into flour. They are most commonly used in Chinese and Indian cookery, but I have used them in a recipe for vegetable pasties.

Lentils are unique among beans, because they require no soaking before they are cooked; this makes them an instant food. Red lentils are often dropped in food parcels to disaster areas because they can be cooked up into a paste or *dal* immediately, providing protein and other valuable nutrients. Lentils are red, yellow, green or brown. I use mainly red and green lentils, and you will find both in recipes in this book – the lentil soufflé is delicious and most unusual.

There are a number of medium-sized white beans that are suitable for general cookery. **Haricots** can be used in a variety of recipes and keep their shape when cooked in casseroles, the most famous of which is the French cassoulet where the beans are used to add to the meat.

Navy beans were the original baked bean and are widely used in North America. **Cannellini beans** are Italian white kidney beans, slightly more elongated than haricot beans, and are often used with tuna fish to make a classic Italian antipasto, although I have used **flageolets** for my tuna bean salad. These are also a member of the kidney bean family, but have an attractive green colour. They are generally available dried and canned, rarely fresh, and are a very good cupboard standby.

Chickpeas, called *chana* in India, are large, pea-shaped beans that are used extensively in Mediterranean, Indian and Middle Eastern cookery. They have a distinctive nutty flavour and are used in casseroles and in dips, the most famous of which is hummus. Chickpeas are a natural partner to sesame seeds and are often used with tahini, a delicious Middle Eastern paste of toasted ground sesame seeds.

ABOVE CHICKEN AND BEAN RISOTTO (SEE PAGE 134)

Other medium-sized beans include **black kidney beans**, used in South American cookery (these are different from the small, round black soya beans, fermented and used in Japanese cookery), and **pinto beans**, which are brown in colour and are the traditional beans used in Mexican dishes, including chilli con carne. They also have the distinction of cooking more quickly than most other beans. Reddish-brown **pink beans** are also used in chilli, particularly in the southern states. **Great Northern beans** are large white beans resembling lima beans in shape but having a more delicate flavour. They grow in the USA midwest and are popular for baked bean dishes. The smaller white **navy beans**, so named because the USA Navy has served them since the 1800s, are widely used in soups and baked beans. **Red kidney beans** are the meat of the kidney bean family: large beans that are widely used because of their colour and

flavour. Kidney beans should always be boiled vigorously for the first ten minutes of their cooking time, in order to destroy any toxins that may be in the beans.

Broad beans, also known as **fava beans**, are large and meaty in texture. **Butter beans**, also called **lima beans**, are usually large and white in colour, and have a sweet, creamy flavour, good for soups and casseroles.

There are two other beans that are less common but worth mentioning. **Ful mesdames** are an Egyptian bean, and a casserole of these beans is to Egypt what roast beef and Yorkshire pudding are to England: a national dish. **Pigeon peas** are similar in size to black-eyed peas or beans, and have a rich earthy flavour. They are widely used throughout the Caribbean and southern USA and are especially favoured for any dish where they are accompanied by rice and a tasty sauce.

Beans and lentils

All dried beans should be soaked before use. Cover with cold water and leave overnight. Make sure you allow soaking time before you prepare a dish containing dried beans. Lentils do not require soaking.

MUNG BEANS

RED LENTILS

CHICKPEAS

BLACK BEANS

KIDNEY BEANS

GREEN LENTILS

HARICOT BEANS

CANNELLINI BEANS

BORLOTTI BEANS

ADZUKI BEANS

BROAD BEANS

Other fibre-rich foods to include in your diet

Dried fruits provide a rich and delicious source of fibre and are excellent for high-fibre desserts.

Pasta is a derivative of wheat and is also a high-fibre food. Wholewheat pasta contains more fibre than others and is becoming widely available in shops.

Nuts are a valuable source of dietary fibre and should always be included in a mixed diet. They are, however, very high in fat, so care should be taken to eat them only in moderation. They typically contain 2 per cent fibre, and 59 per cent fat, so be warned!

Changing to a high-fibre diet

High-fibre eating makes sense when you consider the benefits of eating food in as natural a state as possible. Of course, not every food that you eat has to be high-fibre – you may choose to keep to white pasta but change to wholewheat bread and start eating more fresh fruits, salads and vegetables. As with any eating regime, it is a good idea to eat a wide variety of foods and enjoy them – do not rely just on sprinkling handfuls of bran over everything to increase your fibre intake. This will not be good for your taste buds or for your digestion.

Using the recipes in this book

I have included a wide variety of recipes in this book but, even so, they are really only an introduction to the huge selection of dishes that can be made within the bounds of a high-fibre diet. When you feel confident with a recipe or ingredient, try experimenting for yourself.

Most of the recipes are simple and straightforward. However, high-fibre baking includes more bran and moisture-hungry foods than other baking, so it is advisable to make batters a degree or so wetter than otherwise.

I like to use butter and olive oil in my kitchen at home. In most of these recipes, sunflower margarine can replace the butter, but always use it straight from the refrigerator. You may use your own choice of fat or oil, but always consider the flavour of the finished dish.

A good diet should not only be high in fibre but also low in fat and sugars. Cakes and biscuits should be regarded as treats and not everyday foods, and the amount of extra fat added to foods should be kept to a minimum.

Some of these dishes may be very different from the foods you have been used to eating for many years. I hope you will enjoy trying them, and that you will discover a whole new culinary repertoire that will not only be good for your health, but tempt your taste buds as well.

1

Soups and chowders

A high-fibre soup can easily be a filling meal in itself, so take care when menu planning, especially for a three- or four-course meal. Many of these soups and chowders are made with root vegetables or beans which give a thick texture, especially if the soup is puréed at the end of cooking. Thin the soup if you wish by adding extra stock or milk, but remember that soups are essentially comfort food and many people prefer them thick.

Soups should always be served piping hot or chilled; a tepid soup is a disaster. Do not boil soups that have had single cream or fruit juices, such as orange or lemon, added to them – the cream may curdle and the flavour of the fruit will become tainted. Chilled soups are always better served over crushed ice.

The secret of any successful soup is the flavour of the stock used in its making. Stocks are not difficult to prepare and consist of bones and vegetable peelings, a few herbs and some peppercorns. I collect all my onion skins, carrot scrapings and other clean vegetable waste and place them in a large stockpot with plenty of water, herbs and a light seasoning of salt. Bring to the boil then simmer very slowly for two to three hours, until a rich, dark liquid is produced. Strain the stock then season lightly, to taste. The stock may be reduced to intensify the flavour, in which case it should not be seasoned until it has been boiled. Never cover the pot or the resulting stock may be musty in flavour and cloudy; the stock should be simmered very slowly, with just an occasional bubble breaking the surface.

LEFT SMOKED FISH CHOWDER (SEE PAGE 50)

orange and butternut soup

I FIRST TASTED THIS SOUP ON HOLIDAY IN SOUTH AFRICA. BE CAREFUL NOT TO BOIL THE SOUP AFTER ADDING THE ORANGE JUICE OR THE FLAVOUR WILL BECOME TAINTED. **SERVES 4 TO 6**

1 large onion, chopped

2 tbsp vegetable oil

1 to 2 butternut squashes, weighing about 900 g (2 lb), peeled and diced

Grated rind and juice of 2 oranges

1.5 l (2¾ pts) rich vegetable stock

2 bay leaves

Salt and freshly ground black pepper

Nutmeg, freshly grated

2 tbsp chopped fresh parsley

1 Cook the onion in the oil until softened but not browned, then add the prepared squash and cook slowly for 5 minutes, stirring occasionally. Stir in grated orange rind, then add the stock, bay leaves and seasonings. Bring to the boil, then cover and simmer for 40 minutes, until the squash is tender and cooked through.

2 Allow the soup to cool slightly, remove the bay leaves, then purée in a blender or food processor until smooth. Rinse the pot and return the soup to it, adding the orange juice. Reheat the soup slowly – do not let it boil – then season to taste. Add the chopped parsley and sprinkle with nutmeg just before serving.

sausage, apple and pasta soup

USE CUBED CHEESE INSTEAD OF THE SAUSAGES, AND LET IT MELT INTO THE SOUP. **SERVES 4**

2 tbsp vegetable oil

450 g (1 lb) pork sausages

1 medium onion, finely chopped

1 medium red pepper, seeded
   and chopped

425 ml (¾ pt) dry cider

750 ml (1½ pt) vegetable stock

Salt and freshly ground black pepper

½ tsp nutmeg

100 g (3½ oz) wholewheat macaroni

1 large cooking apple, cored, peeled
   and finely chopped

40 g (1½ oz) grated Cheddar cheese
   (optional)

1 Heat the oil in a large pan, then add the sausages and cook quickly until browned on all sides. Add the onion and pepper and cook more slowly for 3 to 4 minutes, until they are tender.

2 Add the cider and stock to the pan with the seasonings and bring to the boil. Simmer the soup for 30 minutes, then remove the sausages with a slotted spoon. Add the macaroni and simmer for a further 10 to 12 minutes, or until the pasta is just cooked. Slice the sausages while the macaroni is cooking, then return the meat to the pan. Add the apple just before the pasta is cooked – do not simmer it for more than 2 minutes.

3 Season the soup to taste then serve immediately, with or without grated cheese.

artichoke and sweetcorn soup

SWEET AND CREAMY, THIS IS A REAL WINTER WARMER. **SERVES 6**

1 onion, finely chopped

2 tbsp butter

450 g (1 lb) Jerusalem artichokes,
   washed and roughly chopped

250 g (9 oz) frozen sweetcorn

750 ml (1½ pts) rich vegetable stock

Salt and freshly ground black pepper

2 tsp dried red pepper flakes
   (optional)

300 ml (½ pt) milk

3 tbsp soured cream

Freshly chopped chives, for garnish

1 Cook the onion in the butter until soft, then add the artichokes and corn. Stir the vegetables over the heat until the corn starts to defrost, then add the stock and seasonings and bring to the boil. Simmer for 35 to 40 minutes, until the artichokes are tender.

2 Cool the soup slightly, then purée until smooth in a blender or food processor. Rinse the pan and return the soup to it with the milk. Reheat gently, seasoning to taste, then stir in the soured cream and garnish with chopped chives just before serving.

parsnip and apple soup

THE TART APPLE GIVES A REAL PUNCH TO THIS NEW CLASSIC CURRIED PARSNIP SOUP. **SERVES 4 TO 6**

1 large onion, chopped

1 tbsp sunflower oil

1 tsp mild curry powder

450 g (1 lb) parsnips, chopped

1 medium cooking apple, peeled, cored and sliced

1.25 l (2 pts) rich vegetable stock

Salt and freshly ground black pepper

Juice of ½ lemon

Chopped fresh parsley or coriander, to garnish

1 Cook the onion in the oil for 4 to 5 minutes until soft, then stir in the curry powder with the parsnips. Cook for a further 2 to 3 minutes before adding the apple and stock. Bring to the boil, then simmer for 30 minutes or until the parsnip is tender.

2 Allow the soup to cool slightly, then purée until smooth in a blender or food processor. Rinse the pan and return the soup to it, adding sufficient water to thin the soup if necessary. Reheat gently, then season to taste with salt and pepper. Add the lemon juice just before serving and garnish with parsley or coriander.

french onion soup

THE TRADITIONAL FRENCH PICK-ME-UP FOR THE EARLY MORNING AFTER THE NIGHT BEFORE. **SERVES 6**

250 g (9 oz) sliced onions

1 tbsp butter

2 tbsp olive oil

2 tbsp wholewheat flour

750 ml (1½ pts) rich vegetable stock

Salt and freshly ground black pepper

3 bay leaves

4 to 6 slices good wholewheat French bread

40 g (1½ oz) grated Swiss cheese

1 Cook the onions in the butter and oil over high heat in a flameproof casserole dish until softened and well browned; this may take up to 10 minutes. Stir the flour into the onions and cook gently for 1 to 2 minutes. Remove from heat and gradually add the stock, stirring all the time, then season lightly and add the bay leaves. Return the dish to the heat and bring the soup gradually to the boil, cover and simmer for 45 minutes. The soup should be a rich, dark brown colour.

2 Preheat the grill. Remove the bay leaves and season the soup to taste. Fill six individual flameproof serving bowls ⅔ full with soup. Drop a slice of bread into each bowl, then scatter the cheese over the bread. Cook under the hot grill until the cheese has melted and is bubbling. Serve immediately, with a slice of bread in each portion.

broad bean and parsnip chowder

USE SQUASH INSTEAD OF PARSNIP IF YOU PREFER. **SERVES 6**

1 large onion, chopped

2 tbsp oil

1 medium clove garlic

225 g (8 oz) diced parsnip

200 g (7 oz) broad beans, soaked overnight

1 l (1¾ pts) rich vegetable stock

Salt and freshly ground black pepper

Nutmeg, freshly grated

250 ml (9 fl oz) milk

2 slices good wholewheat bread

2 tbsp butter or margarine

1 tbsp chopped fresh parsley

1 Cook the onion in the oil until soft, then add the garlic and parsnip and continue cooking until the parsnip starts to brown. Drain the soaked broad beans and rinse them thoroughly under running water. Add the beans to the pan with the stock, some salt, pepper and nutmeg. Bring the soup to the boil, then cover and simmer slowly for about an hour, until the beans are tender.

2 Allow the soup to cool slightly, then purée it until smooth in a blender or food processor. Rinse the pan and return the soup to it with the milk. Heat gently while preparing the croutons, but do not allow the soup to boil.

3 Toast the bread on one side only. Beat the butter or margarine with a little salt and pepper and the chopped parsley. Spread the mixture over the untoasted side of the bread and cook until lightly browned. Trim away the crusts if you wish, then cut the bread into tiny triangles or squares. Season the soup to taste, and serve with the croutons.

cream of cauliflower and cumin soup

I LOVE THE SUBTLY SPICED FLAVOUR OF THE CAULIFLOWER THAT DOMINATES THIS SOUP. **SERVES 6**

1 tsp cumin seeds

1 medium onion, finely chopped

1 tbsp (15 ml) oil

500 g (1 lb 2 oz) roughly chopped cauliflower, florets and stalks

425 ml (¾ pt) milk

700 ml (1¼ pts) rich vegetable stock

Salt and freshly ground black pepper

1 Heat a dry frying pan until hot, then add the cumin seeds and roast for 1 to 2 minutes. Cool slightly, then grind the seeds to a fine powder in a pestle and mortar or in a bowl with the end of a rolling pin.

2 Cook the onion slowly in the oil until soft but not browned, then add the ground cumin and cauliflower. Continue cooking slowly for 1 to 2 minutes, then add the milk, stock and seasonings. Bring to the boil, then simmer for just 10 minutes. Cool slightly before blending in a blender or food processor until smooth. Rinse the pan, return the soup to it and reheat, seasoning to taste.

minted pea soup

YOUNG PEAS AND FRESH MINT ARE ESSENTIAL, BUT YOU CAN SERVE THE SOUP HOT OR CHILLED OVER CRUSHED ICE, AS YOU PREFER. **SERVES 6**

1 small onion, finely chopped

2 tbsp butter

450 g (1 lb) peas, frozen or, preferably, fresh

2 tbsp chopped fresh mint

1.25 l (2 pts) water

Grated rind of 1 lime

Salt and white pepper to taste

Single cream

1 Cook the onion slowly in the butter until soft but not brown; it is important to soften the onion really well as this soup has a very short cooking time. Stir in the peas and the mint, then add the water and bring the soup to the boil. Simmer for only 3 to 4 minutes, until the peas are just cooked – this will preserve the bright colour of the soup.

2 Cool the soup slightly, then add the lime rind, and purée until smooth in a blender or food processor. Rinse the pot and return the soup to it, seasoning to taste with salt and white pepper. Reheat gently or allow to cool completely before chilling. Serve with a swirl of single cream.

pumpkin and carrot soup

IF LOVAGE IS NOT AVAILABLE, USE CELERY OR FLAT-LEAVED PARSLEY AND OREGANO. **SERVES 8 TO 10**

1 large onion, finely chopped

1 tbsp vegetable oil

450 g (1 lb) carrots, sliced

450 g (1 lb) pumpkin purée, fresh
or tinned

1.5 l (2¾ pts) rich vegetable stock

Salt and freshly ground black pepper

2 tbsp freshly chopped lovage

425 ml (¾ pt) milk

1 tbsp butter or margarine

1 large clove garlic, crushed

2 slices wholewheat bread, toasted

1 Cook the onion in the oil until lightly browned, then add the carrots and cook gently until just softening. Stir in the pumpkin purée, then add the stock and bring to the boil, adding the seasonings and half the lovage. Cover and simmer slowly for 30 to 40 minutes, until the carrots are tender.

2 Allow the soup to cool slightly, then purée until smooth in a blender or food processor. Rinse the pan and return the soup to it with the milk, reheating gently and adding extra seasoning, if required, to taste.

3 Beat the butter and add the remaining lovage and the garlic, then season lightly. Toast the bread, spread it lightly with the butter and cut into small squares or triangles. Drop the toasts into the soup just before serving.

broccoli soup

I PREFER TO USE WATER RATHER THAN STOCK TO ALLOW THE DELICATE BROCCOLI FLAVOUR THROUGH. **SERVES 6**

1 large onion, finely chopped

1 tbsp butter

2 large heads broccoli, weighing
about 450 g (1 lb) in total

Salt and freshly ground black pepper

750 ml (1½ pts) water

425 ml (¾ pt) milk

Grated nutmeg, to taste

Single cream (optional)

1 Cook the onion in the butter until softened but not browned. Trim the broccoli and chop it, using the stalks and the florets. Add the broccoli to the pan, tossing it in the hot juices, then season lightly and add the water. Bring to the boil then simmer for 30 to 40 minutes, until the broccoli is tender.

2 Cool slightly, then purée the soup in a blender or food processor. Rinse the pan and return the soup to it with the milk; heat slowly until almost boiling. Remove from the heat. Season to taste with salt, pepper and nutmeg and serve immediately with a swirl of cream.

chestnut and blue cheese soup

A RICH, SMOKY AND DELICIOUS SOUP. I USE FROZEN CHESTNUTS FOR CONVENIENCE, BUT FRESH OR TINNED WORK JUST AS WELL. **SERVES 6**

1 tbsp vegetable oil

6 to 8 spring onions, trimmed and finely chopped

4 rashers smoked back bacon, chopped

450 g (1 lb) peeled chestnuts, fresh, frozen or tinned; or 225 g (8 oz) dried chestnuts, soaked overnight

750 ml (1½ pts) vegetable stock

2 bay leaves

Salt and freshly ground black pepper

425 ml (¾ pt) milk

125 g (4½ oz) crumbled blue cheese, e.g. Danish or Stilton

Chopped fresh chives, to garnish

1 Heat the oil in a pan, add the spring onions and bacon and cook slowly until the onions are soft. Add the chestnuts, stock and bay leaves with a little salt and pepper. Bring the soup to the boil, cover and simmer for 30 minutes.

2 Remove the bay leaf, allow the soup to cool slightly and purée until smooth in a blender or food processor. Rinse the pan and return the soup to it, then add the milk and return gradually to the boil. Season the soup to taste, then add the crumbled cheese just before serving. Garnish with chopped chives.

tomato, orange and lentil soup

THE ADVANTAGE OF USING LENTILS OVER OTHER BEANS OR LEGUMES IS THAT THEY DON'T REQUIRE SOAKING BEFORE USING. **SERVES 4 TO 6**

1 large onion, finely chopped

1 tbsp vegetable oil

Grated rind and juice of 1 large orange

100 g (3½ oz) red lentils

400 g (14 oz) tin chopped tomatoes

750 ml (1½ pts) rich vegetable stock

Salt and freshly ground black pepper

A few small basil leaves

1 Cook the onion in the oil until soft then add the orange rind and lentils. Quickly stir in the chopped tomatoes, add the stock and a little seasoning. Bring the soup to the boil and simmer for 30 minutes, until the lentils are soft.

2 Allow the soup to cool slightly, add half the basil, then purée until smooth in a blender or food processor. Rinse the pan and return the soup to it, adding the orange juice and the remaining basil leaves, torn into small pieces. Heat the soup gently – do not allow it to boil after adding the orange juice or the flavour will be tainted. Season to taste and serve with crusty bread.

beetroot soup with horseradish

A LIGHTER VARIATION ON CLASSIC RUSSIAN BORSCHT, THIS PEPPERY
SOUP IS DELICIOUS – BUT TAKE CARE THAT YOUR BEETROOT HAS NOT
BEEN DRESSED IN VINEGAR BEFORE USE OR YOUR SOUP WILL TASTE
HORRIBLE! FRESH BEETROOT IS BEST. **SERVES 6**

1 large onion, finely chopped

2 medium white turnips, diced

1 tbsp vegetable oil

450 g (1 lb) cooked beetroot, diced

1.5 l (2¾ pts) rich vegetable or beef stock

Salt and freshly ground black pepper

4 bay leaves

2 tsp grated horseradish

1 tbsp freshly chopped chives

150 ml (¼ pt) soured cream

1 Cook the onion and the turnip in the oil until softened but not browned, then add the beetroot and the stock and bring to the boil. Reduce the heat, add the seasonings, bay leaves, and a teaspoon of the horseradish, cover and simmer for 30 to 40 minutes.

2 Allow the soup to cool slightly and remove the bay leaves. Then purée until smooth in a blender or food processor. Rinse the pan and return the soup to it and reheat the soup gently. Mix the remaining horseradish and most of the chives into the soured cream. Season the soup to taste and serve with a large dollop of the flavoured soured cream in each portion, topped with chives.

fennel and walnut soup

THIS ANISEED-FLAVOURED SOUP IS A DINNER PARTY FAVOURITE. **SERVES 4 TO 6**

1 large onion, finely chopped

1 large bulb fennel, trimmed and sliced

3 sticks celery, trimmed and sliced

2 tbsp vegetable oil

1 plump garlic clove, finely sliced

2 bay leaves

1.4 l (2¼ pts) vegetable stock

Salt and freshly ground black pepper

150 ml (¼ pt) soured cream or plain yoghurt

50 g (1¾ oz) walnuts, finely chopped

Chopped fresh parsley mixed with fennel fronds and celery leaves, to garnish

1 Cook the prepared vegetables slowly in the oil until soft but not browned. Add the garlic, bay leaves and stock, and bring the soup to the boil. Cover the pan and simmer for 30 to 40 minutes, until the vegetables are tender.

2 Cool the soup slightly and remove bay leaves. Purée until smooth in a blender or food processor. Rinse the pan and return the soup to it. Reheat gently and season to taste with salt and pepper, then stir in the soured cream or yoghurt. Add the walnuts just before serving and garnish with any reserved chopped fennel fronds, the celery leaves and parsley.

spinach and courgette soup

THIS SOUP HAS A STRONG, WARMING, PEPPERY FLAVOUR. **SERVES 8**

1 small onion, finely chopped

1 tbsp oil

1 to 2 cloves garlic, crushed

450 g (1 lb) fresh (washed) or frozen spinach

2 medium courgettes, trimmed and grated

1.5 l (2¾ pts) rich vegetable stock

Salt and freshly ground black pepper

Grated nutmeg, to taste

1 tbsp fresh basil leaves, roughly torn

Grated courgette and wholewheat croutons, to garnish

1 Cook the onion in the oil until soft then add the garlic, spinach and courgettes. Mix well, then stir in the stock and bring the soup to the boil. Season lightly with salt, pepper and nutmeg, and simmer for 20 minutes.

2 Allow the soup to cool slightly, add the basil leaves and purée until smooth in a blender or food processor. Rinse the pan and return the soup to it. Reheat gently, adding extra seasoning to taste, and serve the soup garnished with raw grated courgette and wholewheat croutons.

mexican bean soup

PINTO BEANS ARE TRADITIONAL, BUT IF YOU CAN'T GET THEM, USE EXTRA
KIDNEY BEANS INSTEAD. **SERVES 6**

100 g (3½ oz) red kidney beans, soaked overnight

100 g (3½ oz) pinto beans, soaked overnight

1 large onion, finely chopped

1 tbsp oil

1 red chilli, seeded and finely chopped

1 large clove garlic, finely sliced

1 tsp mild chilli powder

1 tbsp coriander leaves

1.5 l (2¾ pts) rich vegetable stock

1 tbsp tomato purée

Salt and freshly ground black pepper

40 g (1½ oz) Cheddar cheese, grated

Guacamole for serving, see page 95

1 Drain the beans and rinse them thoroughly under cold running water; set aside until needed. Cook the onion in the oil until soft, add the chilli, garlic and chilli powder, and cook for another minute.

2 Stir the beans into the pan, then add the coriander, stock, tomato purée and seasonings. Bring the soup to the boil and cook for 10 minutes, then simmer slowly for 45 to 60 minutes, until the beans are soft. Allow the soup to cool, and purée until smooth in a blender or food processor. Rinse the pan then return the soup to it and reheat gently, seasoning to taste with salt and pepper. Scatter the cheese over the soup just before serving and set out a dish of guacamole.

armenian soup

THIS SPICY LENTIL SOUP IS SWEETENED AND THICKENED WITH APRICOTS AND SULTANAS. **SERVES 6**

1 large onion, finely chopped

2 tbsp olive oil

1 tsp ground ginger

1 tsp ground cumin

½ tsp ground cinnamon

2 medium tomatoes, diced

175 g (6 oz) red lentils

1.5 l (2¾ pts) rich vegetable stock

Salt and freshly ground black pepper

100 g (3½ oz) ready-to-eat dried apricots, roughly chopped

50 g (1¾ oz) sultanas

Soured cream or plain yoghurt (optional)

1 Cook the onion in the oil in a large pan until soft, add the spices and cook for 1 minute over low heat. Add the tomatoes and lentils, stir in the stock and slowly bring the soup to the boil. Season well, add the dried fruit, cover and simmer for 30 minutes, until the lentils and vegetables are soft.

2 Season the soup to taste. It may be puréed if preferred, then thinned down with a little extra stock or water. Serve with a dollop of soured cream or yoghurt.

gazpacho

THIS IS THE CLASSIC COLD TOMATO SOUP OF SPAIN – AND THE TRICK
IS TO CHILL IT REALLY WELL. **SERVES 8**

½ cucumber, chopped

1 medium green pepper, seeded and finely chopped

1 medium red onion, finely chopped

3 medium cloves garlic, crushed

50 g (1¾ oz) fresh white breadcrumbs

Three 400 g (14 oz) tins chopped tomatoes

Salt

50 ml (2 fl oz) white wine vinegar

50 ml (2 fl oz) fruity olive oil

300 ml (½ pt) water or vegetable stock

Sugar

GARNISH

1 small green pepper, seeded and finely chopped

½ cucumber, seeded and finely chopped

1 small red onion, finely chopped

Crushed ice if available

1 Purée all the soup ingredients together in a blender or food
processor, adding as much water or stock as necessary to make a
thick, smooth creamy soup. Season well, adding sugar to taste, then
chill the soup with about 12 ice cubes until very cold. The soup
will become slightly more liquid as the ice melts in it.

2 Prepare the garnishes for the soup and serve them in small
bowls. Serve each helping of soup over half a cup of crushed ice
to keep it chilled, or as here, straight from the fridge.

minestrone

THERE ARE MANY RECIPES FOR THIS CLASSIC DISH. THIS VERSION IS THICKENED WITH BOTH LENTILS AND SPAGHETTI AND MAKES A HEARTY STARTER. **SERVES 8**

1 large onion, finely chopped

1 large leek, trimmed and finely sliced

4 rashers smoked back bacon, finely diced

2 tbsp olive oil

125 g (4½ oz) finely diced carrot

75 g (2¾ oz) red lentils

Two 400 g (14 oz) tins chopped tomatoes

750 ml (1½ pts) rich vegetable or chicken stock

2 tbsp freshly chopped herbs

Salt and freshly ground black pepper

50 g (1¾ oz) shredded cabbage

50 g (1¾ oz) broken wholewheat spaghetti

2 to 3 tbsp pesto

1 Cook the onion, leek and bacon in the oil until softened but not browned, then stir in the carrot and cook for a further 1 to 2 minutes. Add the lentils, tomatoes, stock, herbs and seasonings and bring to the boil; cover the pan and simmer for 20 minutes.

2 Add the cabbage and spaghetti, return the soup to the boil, then simmer for a further 10 minutes. Season to taste, stir in the pesto and serve immediately.

mulligatawny soup

MULLIGATAWNY COMES FROM THE TAMIL WORD "PEPPER WATER"; BEFORE CHILLIES WERE WIDELY AVAILABLE IN ASIA ALL THE HEAT IN CURRIES CAME FROM PEPPERCORNS. **SERVES 4 TO 6**

2 medium onions, finely sliced

3 tbsp vegetable oil

1 chicken (about 1.4 kg/3 lb) jointed and skinned

1 to 2 tbsp mild curry powder, according to taste

½ tsp ground cloves

150 ml (¼ pt) plain yoghurt

1.5 l (2¾ pts) water

1 tsp salt

Freshly ground black pepper

125 g (4½ oz) cooked rice

1 red eating apple, cored and diced

Juice of ½ lemon

1 Cook the onion in the oil until soft then add the chicken pieces. Continue to cook over moderate heat until browned all over. Add the curry powder and ground cloves and cook for a further 1 minute, stir in the yoghurt and heat until the yoghurt has loosened any sediment from the bottom of the pot. Add the water to the pan with the salt and pepper, bring to the boil and simmer, covered, for 1 hour, or until the chicken begins to fall off the bone.

2 Remove the chicken, take the meat from the bone and return it to the pan with the cooked rice. Toss the apple in the lemon juice, add that to the pan, and return the soup to the boil. Simmer for 2 to 3 minutes, season to taste and serve.

ABOVE THAI-SPICED CHICKEN CHOWDER

lebanese couscous soup

IN THIS RECIPE, COUSCOUS – TINY GRAINS MADE FROM SEMOLINA – IS USED TO THICKEN THE RICHLY SPICED ONION SOUP. **SERVES 6**

4 large onions, finely sliced

3 medium cloves garlic, finely sliced

2 tbsp vegetable oil

1 tbsp butter

1 small red chilli, seeded and finely chopped

1 tsp mild chilli powder

½ tsp ground turmeric

1 tsp ground coriander

2 l (3½ pts) rich vegetable or chicken stock

Salt and freshly ground black pepper

50 g (1¾ oz) couscous

Chopped fresh coriander, to garnish

1 Cook the onions and garlic in the oil and butter until well browned. This will take about 15 minutes over medium high heat. You must let the onions brown to achieve a rich colour for the finished soup.

2 Stir in the chopped chilli and the spices and cook over low heat for a further 1 to 2 minutes before adding the stock. Season lightly then bring to the boil. Cover and simmer for 30 minutes.

3 Stir the couscous into the soup, return to the boil and simmer for a further 10 minutes. Season to taste then garnish with coriander and serve immediately.

thai-spiced chicken chowder

PEEL THE LEMON GRASS AND BRUISE SLIGHTLY BEFORE FINELY CHOPPING. **SERVES 4**

1 to 2 tbsp peanut or sunflower oil

2 small, boneless chicken breasts, skinned and shredded

2 tsp Thai 7-Spice seasoning

1 stick lemon grass, finely chopped

2 medium potatoes, diced

700 ml (1¼ pts) chicken or vegetable stock

425 ml (¾ pt) milk

3 to 4 spring onions, trimmed and finely sliced

125 g (4½ oz) frozen or fresh peas

1 to 2 tbsp satay sauce or peanut butter

Salt and freshly ground black pepper

Double cream, to garnish (optional)

1 Heat the oil in a large pan; add the chicken and 7-Spice seasoning and cook quickly until the chicken begins to brown. Stir in the lemon grass and potato, then add the liquids. Bring the chowder slowly to the boil, cover and simmer for 20 minutes.

2 Stir the spring onions into the chowder with the peas; return to the boil and continue cooking for a further 5 minutes.

3 Add the satay sauce to the chowder just before serving. Remove from heat and stir until melted. Season to taste and serve, garnished with a spoonful of cream if desired.

chicken and bean chowder

THIS MAKES FOR A MEAL IN ITSELF WHEN SERVED WITH CRUSTY BREAD AND A FRESH
GREEN SALAD. **SERVES 6**

2 tbsp olive oil

2 medium chicken thighs

1 large onion, finely chopped

**1 medium green pepper, seeded and
cut into strips**

**1 small red chilli, seeded and finely
chopped**

2 small cloves garlic, crushed

1 tbsp chopped fresh oregano

**1 tbsp chopped fresh flat-leafed
parsley**

400-g (14-oz) tin chopped tomatoes

2 tbsp tomato purée

**1.25 l (2 pts) rich chicken or
vegetable stock**

Salt and freshly ground black pepper

**425-g (15-oz) tin borlotti beans or
mixed pulses, drained and rinsed**

**Chopped fresh parsley and Parmesan
cheese, to garnish**

1 Heat the oil in a large pan; add the chicken and brown all over. Remove the chicken from the pan with a slotted spoon and set aside. Stir the onion into the pan juices and cook until softened but not browned. Add the pepper, chilli, garlic and herbs and stir well. Add the tomatoes, tomato purée and stock. Return the chicken to the pan, season lightly and bring the soup to the boil. Cover and simmer for 40 to 50 minutes, until the chicken is cooked.

2 Remove the chicken from the pan and take the meat from the bones. Shred the chicken and return it to the pan with the beans. Return the soup to the boil and simmer for 3 to 4 minutes to heat the beans thoroughly.

3 Season the soup to taste and garnish with extra parsley. Slivers of Parmesan cheese may be sprinkled into the soup before serving.

squash chowder

USE ANY HARD-SKINNED SQUASH FOR THIS CHOWDER. **SERVES 6**

350 g (12 oz) squash, diced finely

2 rashers smoked back bacon, finely chopped

2 tbsp fruity olive oil

4 to 5 sprigs fresh thyme

2 bay leaves

750 ml (1½ pts) rich vegetable stock

Salt and freshly ground black pepper

100 g (3½ oz) cabbage, finely shredded

60 g (2 oz) creamed coconut

250 ml (9 fl oz) milk

1 large tomato, finely diced

125 g (4½ oz) frozen or fresh prawns (optional)

1 tbsp white wine vinegar

Chopped fresh parsley, to garnish

1 Cook the squash and the bacon in the oil in a heavy pan for 6 to 8 minutes, stirring frequently, until the squash is beginning to soften. Add the herbs and stock, season lightly and bring to the boil. Reduce the heat and simmer for 10 minutes, then add the cabbage and creamed coconut and continue cooking for a further 10 to 15 minutes.

2 Remove the thyme and bay leaves, then add the milk and the chopped tomato with the prawns, if desired. Return the chowder to the boil and cook for a further 5 minutes. Season to taste, then add the vinegar and parsley just before serving.

smoked fish chowder

FIRM-FLESHED SMOKED FISH MAKES AN EXCELLENT CHOWDER.

SERVES 6

425 ml (¾ pt) milk

250 g (8 oz) smoked haddock or other white fish fillet, skinned

1 tbsp butter

1 small onion, finely chopped

2 sticks celery, finely chopped

2 medium potatoes, diced

425 ml (¾ pt) fish stock or water

125 g (4½ oz) frozen or fresh peas

125 g (4½ oz) frozen sweetcorn

Salt and freshly ground black pepper

2 tbsp chopped fresh parsley

1 Heat the milk in a frying pan until almost boiling, then add the haddock and poach for 4 to 5 minutes. Remove the haddock with a slotted spoon and reserve the milk.

2 Melt the butter in a separate pan, add the onion and celery and cook slowly until soft. Stir in the diced potato, stock and the reserved milk, and bring to the boil. Reduce the heat and simmer the soup for 15 minutes, until the potato is tender.

3 Add the peas and sweetcorn and return the soup to the boil. Flake the haddock and add it to the chowder, then continue to cook for a further 2 to 3 minutes, until the peas and sweetcorn are tender and the fish is hot.

4 Season the chowder to taste and stir in half the parsley. Garnish with the remaining parsley and serve.

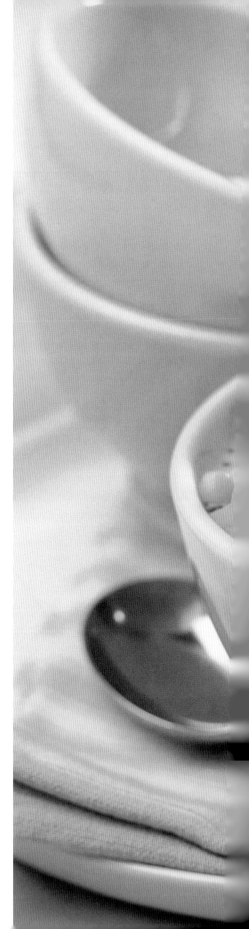

buckwheat and mushroom soup

BUCKWHEAT HAS A STRONG, SLIGHTLY SWEET AND FRAGRANTLY NUTTY FLAVOUR. ONLY A LITTLE IS REQUIRED IN ORDER NOT TO OVERPOWER THE MUSHROOMS. **SERVES 6**

25 g (1 oz) dried porcini mushrooms

150 ml (¼ pt) sherry

1 tbsp butter

1 tbsp olive oil

1 large onion, finely chopped

2 sticks celery, finely chopped

2 rashers smoked back bacon, finely chopped

250 g (9 oz) roughly chopped mushrooms

2 plump cloves garlic, finely sliced

50 g (1¾ oz) raw buckwheat groats

1.25 l (2 pts) rich vegetable stock

Salt and freshly ground black pepper

Nutmeg, freshly grated

300 ml (½ pt) milk

Cream and paprika, to garnish

1 Soak the porcinis in the sherry for at least 30 minutes before starting the soup. Heat the butter and the oil together then add the onion, celery, and bacon and cook slowly for about 5 minutes, until the vegetables have softened but not browned. Add the chopped mushrooms and garlic and cook slowly for a further 2 to 3 minutes, until the juices start to run from the mushrooms. Add the porcinis and the sherry, then stir in the buckwheat and pour in the stock.

2 Bring the soup slowly to the boil, stirring up any scrapings from the bottom of the pot. Season lightly with salt, pepper, and nutmeg, then cover the pot and simmer the soup for 40 minutes.

3 Allow the soup to cool slightly then purée until smooth in a blender or food processor. Rinse the pot and return the soup to it with the milk. Reheat gently, then season to taste. Garnish with a swirl of cream and a little paprika.

crab and sweetcorn soup

THIS IS A CLASSIC CHINESE SOUP WITH A CREAMY, FRAGRANT COMBINATION OF FLAVOURS. **SERVES 6**

425-g (15-oz) tin creamed sweetcorn

250-g (8-oz) tin or fresh crab meat

1.25 l (2 pts) rich fish, chicken or vegetable stock

Salt and freshly ground black pepper

1 tbsp soy sauce

2 egg whites

4 to 6 spring onions, shredded

1 Bring the corn, crab meat, stock, seasoning and soy sauce to the boil in a large pot, stirring to mix the corn and the crab evenly throughout the soup. Simmer for 10 minutes.

2 Whisk the egg whites into soft peaks, then stir carefully into the soup just before serving. Garnish with spring onions.

chickpea soup with red pepper salsa

DON'T BE PUT OFF BY THE NUMBER OF INGREDIENTS – THIS IS A LIGHTLY SPICED, CREAMY SOUP WITH A ZINGY
SALSA GARNISH – DELICIOUS! **SERVES 6**

125 g (4½ oz) chickpeas, soaked
    overnight or tinned

1 tsp cumin seeds

½ tsp mustard seeds, preferably white

1 tbsp sesame seeds

1 large onion, finely sliced

1 tbsp olive oil

2 large cloves garlic, finely sliced

½ tsp dry ground ginger

750 ml (1½ pts) rich stock

Salt and freshly ground black pepper

300 ml (½ pt) milk

SALSA

½ small red pepper, chopped

¼ cucumber, chopped

½ small red onion, finely chopped

1 medium clove garlic, finely chopped

1 small tomato, chopped

1 small red chilli, seeded and
    finely chopped

1 to 2 tbsp coriander leaves,
    finely torn

Grated rind and juice of 1 lemon

1 to 2 tbsp soured cream (optional)

1 Drain the chickpeas and rinse them thoroughly under cold running water; set aside. Heat a non-stick frying pan until evenly hot, add the cumin, mustard and sesame seeds and roast for 2 to 3 minutes, until they start to pop. Transfer the spices to a mortar or a spice mill and grind until smooth. You may also use the end of a rolling pin to grind them.

2 Cook the onion in the oil in a large pan until well browned, then add the garlic, ginger and freshly ground spices and cook slowly for another minute. Stir in the chickpeas and the stock and bring the soup to the boil; season lightly. Simmer for 45 to 60 minutes, until the chickpeas are soft.

3 Prepare the salsa while the soup is cooking. Mix together all the prepared vegetables, season lightly and add the coriander, lemon rind and lemon juice. Allow the salsa to stand for at least 30 minutes for the flavours to blend together.

4 Allow the soup to cool slightly, then purée in a blender or food processor until smooth. Rinse the pan and return the soup to it, reheat gently with the milk, seasoning with salt and pepper to taste. Blend the salsa with one to two tablespoons of soured cream, if wished, and serve the soup with a generous spoonful of salsa over each portion.

roasted pumpkin and smoked mussel soup

IF YOU CANNOT FIND SMOKED MUSSELS, WARMED SMOKED MACKEREL WILL MAKE A
DELICIOUS SUBSTITUTE. **SERVES 6**

½ small pumpkin or 1 medium firm-
fleshed squash

Freshly ground black pepper

3 tbsp olive oil

1 medium leek, finely sliced

2 sticks celery, trimmed and sliced

1 small carrot, sliced

2 tsp ground coriander

3 to 4 sprigs fresh thyme

1 bay leaf

750 ml (1½ pts) rich vegetable stock

425 ml (¾ pt) milk

Salt

150 g (5½ oz) smoked mussels

Chopped fresh parsley

1 Preheat oven to 220°C/425°F/Gas 7. Cut the pumpkin into slices about 4 to 5 cm (1½ to 2 in) wide and place them in a roasting tin. You will need 6 slices. Season lightly with pepper then brush the flesh with olive oil. Bake in the preheated oven for about 30 minutes, until the pumpkin is tender. Scoop the flesh from the skin and place to one side.

2 Heat two tablespoons of olive oil in a large pan; add the leek, celery and carrot and cook slowly until soft. Stir in the ground coriander and cook slowly for a further minute. Add the pumpkin flesh to the pan with the thyme and bay leaf, then pour in the stock. Bring the soup to the boil, cover and simmer slowly for 35 to 40 minutes.

3 Allow the soup to cool slightly then purée until smooth in a blender or food processor. Rinse the pan, then return the soup to it with the milk and bring slowly to simmering point. Season well with salt and pepper, add the smoked mussels and heat for another minute or two. Serve garnished with parsley.

leek and spinach barley soup

LEEKS GREW WILD IN IRELAND FOR MANY CENTURIES. HERE THEY ADD
TO THE TRADITIONAL FLAVOUR OF THIS WARMING SOUP. **SERVES 6**

300 g (10½ oz) finely sliced leeks

2 tbsp olive oil

25 g (1 oz) shredded spinach

50 g (1¾ oz) pearl barley

1.5 l (2¾ pts) rich chicken or vegetable stock

1 bouquet garni

Salt and freshly ground black pepper

2 bay leaves

50 ml (2 fl oz) double cream (optional)

1 Cook the leeks in the oil until softened but not browned, then
add the spinach and cook briefly until wilted. Add the barley,
stock and bouquet garni, and bring to the boil. Season lightly, add
the bay leaves, then cover the pot and simmer for about 1½ hours,
until the barley is tender.

2 Remove the bouquet garni and bay leaves. Season to taste,
then stir in the cream, if used, and serve immediately with
fresh crusty bread.

2 Salads and starters

Many of the salads included in this section are suitable as a side dish or as a main course with hot potatoes or crusty bread. If you are planning to serve a salad as a main course you will usually need to double the quantities.

Salads have come a long way in the last few years, and designer lettuces and other unusual greens offer all sorts of presentation opportunities for the home cook. While the appearance of a salad is very important, the selection of the ingredients, which should all be at the very peak of their ripeness, is paramount. It is impossible to make a good salad from limp lettuce, underripe tomatoes and a hard, tasteless strawberry added for a touch of sophistication. Some of the best salads are made from the simplest of ingredients, all packed with flavour. The Spinach Salad included here is an excellent example of a very simple dish based on fresh and flavourful ingredients: young spinach and sun-ripened tomatoes.

I always like to use a full-flavoured home-made dressing for my salads, usually made with a fruity extra-virgin olive oil. I use sherry vinegar and a generous amount of mustard, balanced with sugar, salt and pepper. Taste the dressing, then keep adding seasonings until it is right.

Starters should always be small and fairly light. They should stimulate the appetite for what is to follow and never be too filling or too heavy. Do not serve a very heavily seasoned dish before a delicate main course, which may seem bland in comparison, but try to pick dishes that complement each other.

LEFT CRUNCHY CORN SALAD (SEE PAGE 64)

pasta salad

USE WHITE PASTA IF YOU PREFER: THERE IS PLENTY OF FIBRE IN THE VEGETABLES AND BEANS. **SERVES 12 AS A STARTER, 6 TO 8 AS A MAIN COURSE**

250 g (8 oz) wholewheat pasta of your choice

1 medium red pepper, seeded and diced

125 g (4½ oz) button mushrooms, halved

½ cucumber, diced

175 g (6 oz) sweetcorn

6 spring onions, finely sliced

425-g (15-oz) tin red kidney beans, drained and rinsed

100 g (3½ oz) diced Swiss cheese

Salt and freshly ground black pepper

DRESSING

350 g (12 oz) strained cottage cheese or plain yoghurt

225 g (8 oz) mayonnaise

Salt and freshly ground black pepper

2 to 3 cloves garlic, crushed

15 g (½ oz) chopped fresh chives

Salad greens, to serve

1 Bring a large pan of salted water to the boil and add the pasta. Return to the boil, then simmer as directed until just tender. Drain the pasta and rinse it in cold water, then let cool completely.

2 Mix all the prepared vegetables together and season lightly with salt and pepper. Blend all the ingredients for the dressing and season to taste.

3 Place the pasta in a large bowl, then top with the vegetables. Spoon on the dressing. If the salad is prepared in advance, I suggest leaving it in layers and tossing at the last minute. If it is to be served immediately, however, toss all the ingredients together then transfer the salad to a large platter, lined with salad greens.

roasted chicory and pink grapefruit salad

I LOVE CHICORY, BUT I PREFER IT COOKED TO RAW. HERE IT IS SET OFF BY THE ZING OF THE GRAPEFRUIT. **SERVES 4**

2 heads chicory, trimmed

1 tbsp finely chopped onion

Salt and freshly ground black pepper

1 tbsp olive oil

40 g (1½ oz) pine kernels

2 medium tomatoes, halved and sliced

1 small ruby grapefruit, peeled and cut into segments

1 to 2 tbsp chopped fresh chives

Salt and freshly ground black pepper

1 to 2 tbsp fruity olive oil

1 Preheat the oven to220°C/425°F/Gas 7. Cut the chicory in half lengthways and place in a roasting tin. Scatter the onion over top, season well and drizzle with the oil. Roast in the preheated oven for 15 minutes, then allow to cool.

2 Toast the pine kernels in a hot dry frying pan for 3 to 4 minutes until browned, then allow to cool.

3 Slice the roasted chicory and mix it with the pine kernels, tomatoes, grapefruit and chives. Season well, spoon the olive oil over, then serve on a bed of lettuce or raw spinach.

classic waldorf salad

MIXING YOGHURT WITH MAYONNAISE MAKES A MUCH MILDER DRESSING FOR THE SALAD. **SERVES 6 TO 8**

2 crisp, red eating apples, cored and diced

2 green eating apples, cored and diced

Juice of 1 lemon

1 head celery, trimmed and sliced

200 g (7 oz) chopped walnuts

Salt and freshly ground black pepper

225 g (8 oz) plain yoghurt

100 g (3½ oz) mayonnaise

Lettuce leaves

Paprika

1 Toss the diced apples in the lemon juice to prevent them from browning. Mix the apples with the celery and walnuts and season well.

2 Blend the yoghurt and mayonnaise together, then spoon over the salad. Toss until all the ingredients are evenly coated; add extra mayonnaise if necessary.

3 Line a bowl with lettuce leaves, then arrange the salad in the bowl. Sprinkle a little paprika over the salad just before serving.

pear and grape salad

THIS SALAD OFFERS A DELICIOUS COMBINATION OF TASTES AND TEXTURES. **SERVES 4**

2 Little Gem lettuces, torn into bite-sized pieces

1 head chicory, trimmed and sliced

2 large ripe dessert pears, sliced

Juice of ½ lemon

100 g (3½ oz) grapes, preferably black, halved and seeded

125 ml (4 fl oz) soured cream

75 g (2¾ oz) low-fat cream cheese

1 to 2 cloves garlic, crushed

Salt and freshly ground black pepper

Paprika

1 Mix together the lettuce and chicory and arrange in a salad bowl or on individual plates. Toss the pears in the lemon juice, arrange the pieces over the lettuce and add the grapes.

2 Blend together the soured cream and cream cheese, add the garlic and season well with salt and pepper. Spoon the dressing into the centre of the salad, garnish with paprika, then serve with fresh, crusty wholewheat bread.

crunchy corn salad

IF YOU PREFER, BLANCH THE BEAN SPROUTS BEFORE ADDING THEM
TO THE SALAD. **SERVES 4**

125 g (4 oz) fresh corn, cut from the cob

125 g (4 oz) mange tout, trimmed and shredded

1 medium courgette, trimmed and cut into matchsticks

1 large carrot, cut into matchsticks

2 pieces preserved stem ginger, chopped

200 g (7 oz) bean sprouts

2 tbsp sesame seeds, toasted

Salt and freshly ground black pepper

DRESSING

2 tbsp clear honey

1 tbsp sesame oil

Grated rind and juice of 1 lime

2 tbsp ginger syrup (from the bottle of preserved ginger)

2 tbsp light soy sauce

1 Blanch the corn in a large pan of water for just 2 minutes, then add the mange tout and cook for 1 minute. Drain the vegetables, then plunge immediately into cold water. Drain again when cold.

2 Combine the blanched vegetables with the courgette and carrot, ginger and bean sprouts, then add the sesame seeds.

3 Whisk together all the ingredients for the dressing and season to taste with salt and pepper. Pour the dressing over the salad vegetables and toss thoroughly before serving.

buckwheat salad

BUCKWHEAT IS USED EXTENSIVELY IN EASTERN EUROPEAN COOKERY. ROASTING THE GROATS BRINGS OUT THE NUTTY FLAVOUR. **SERVES 6 TO 8**

250 g (9 oz) buckwheat groats, roasted or raw

750 ml (1½ pts) rich vegetable stock

3 tbsp vinaigrette

150 g (5½ oz) diced carrot

¼ cucumber, diced

50 g (1¾ oz) diced pickled cucumbers

75 g (2¾ oz) poppy seeds

25 g (1 oz) chopped fresh parsley (optional)

Salt and freshly ground black pepper

1 Bring the buckwheat and stock to the boil, cover the pan and simmer for 30 to 35 minutes until the stock has been absorbed and the groats are tender. Drain any excess liqiud. Stir in the vinaigrette, then leave to cool completely.

2 Add all the remaining ingredients to the buckwheat and mix well, seasoning to taste. Serve at room temperature.

brown rice salad with fruit and seeds

TRY ADDING STRAWBERRIES WHEN THEY ARE IN SEASON. **SERVES 6**

250 g (9 oz) brown rice

40 g (1½ oz) sunflower seeds

25 g (1 oz) sesame seeds

50 g (1¾ oz) pumpkin seeds

6 spring onions, trimmed and sliced

1 large mango, peeled and diced

50 g (1¾ oz) dried cranberries

DRESSING

Grated rind and juice of 1 lemon

2 tbsp clear honey

4 tbsp sunflower or peanut oil

1 tbsp dill weed, chopped

Salt and freshly ground black pepper

1 Bring the rice to the boil in a large pan of cold water and simmer for 20 to 25 minutes until the rice is just tender but not soggy.

2 Prepare the dressing while the rice is cooking. Whisk together all the ingredients, seasoning to taste with salt and pepper. Drain the rice well, shake gently, then transfer it to a large bowl and add the dressing. Toss well and leave until the rice has cooled, tossing from time to time.

3 Toast the sunflower seeds in a dry frying pan for 2 to 3 minutes until they begin to brown, then add the sesame seeds and cook for a further 1 to 2 minutes. Allow to cool, then add the pumpkin seeds.

4 Toss the cooled rice with the seeds, spring onions and fruit. Add a little extra seasoning if necessary and garnish with more dill just before serving.

cucumber tabbouleh

IT IS IMPORTANT TO DRY THE BULGUR THOROUGHLY OR THE FINISHED SALAD WILL BE SOGGY. **SERVES 6**

150 g (5½ oz) bulgur

425 ml (¾ pt) boiling water

15 g (½ oz) chopped fresh parsley

15 g (½ oz) chopped fresh mint

2 medium tomatoes, seeded and chopped

2 spring onions, trimmed and finely chopped

½ cucumber, diced

Juice of 1 lime

Salt and freshly ground black pepper

50 ml (2 fl oz) fruity olive oil

1 Allow the bulgur to soak in boiling water for 30 minutes, then drain, and squeeze dry in a clean teatowel.

2 Place the bulgur in a large bowl and add all the remaining ingredients, including seasonings to taste. Toss the salad well and serve at room temperature.

cracked wheat salad

SLICE THE VEGETABLES QUITE FINELY SO THAT THEY DO NOT
CONTRAST TOO MUCH WITH THE WHEAT. **SERVES 6 TO 8**

150 g (5½ oz) cracked wheat

425 ml (¾ pt) boiling water

40 g (1½ oz) pumpkin seeds

1 small green pepper, seeded and finely chopped

2 sticks celery, finely sliced

1 small leek, trimmed and finely sliced

½ small cucumber, finely diced

50 g (1¾ oz) chopped fresh parsley

15 g (½ oz) chopped fresh mixed herbs

DRESSING

Grated rind and juice of 1 lime

50 ml (2 fl oz) fruity extra-virgin olive oil

Salt and freshly ground black pepper

1 Place the cracked wheat in a bowl, pour the boiling water over and leave for at least 30 minutes. Drain in a sieve, then wring excess water out in a clean teatowel.

2 Place the cracked wheat in a bowl with the seeds and prepared vegetables. Season lightly.

3 Whisk the dressing ingredients until blended, then pour it over the salad. Top with a layer of the freshly chopped herbs, all mixed together. Toss all the ingredients just before serving.

date and pear cottage cheese salad

THE ADVANTAGE OF COTTAGE CHEESE OVER OTHER CHEESES IS THAT IT IS LOW IN FAT. **SERVES 4**

200 g (7 oz) cottage cheese

75 g (2¾ oz) stoned dates, chopped

2 firm dessert pears

Juice of 1 lemon

2 small oranges

2 heads chicory, trimmed and sliced

Salt and freshly ground black pepper

Watercress or rocket leaves

1 Place the cottage cheese in a bowl and add the dates. Core and dice the pears and toss with the lemon juice. Peel the oranges and cut the rind into thin strips for garnish. Remove any seeds, then roughly chop the oranges. Add the pears to the cottage cheese with the oranges and chicory. Season to taste with salt and pepper.

2 Line a suitable bowl or platter with watercress or rocket leaves, then arrange the salad in the middle. Garnish with the reserved orange rind before serving.

beetroot and sorrel salad

ADD THE BEETROOT JUST BEFORE SERVING TO PREVENT THE COLOUR FROM BLEEDING INTO THE OTHER INGREDIENTS. **SERVES 4**

Salad greens

1 small bunch watercress, trimmed, washed and shaken dry

40 g (1½ oz) shredded young sorrel or spinach leaves

150 g (5½ oz) shredded celeriac or thinly sliced celery

Grated rind and juice of 1 lemon

4 small beetroot, cooked and diced

DRESSING

4 tbsp fruity olive oil

1 tbsp sherry vinegar

½ tsp sugar

1 tbsp Dijon mustard

Salt and freshly ground black pepper

1 Arrange the salad leaves in a bowl or on a platter, then add the watercress and sorrel and mix well. Toss the celeriac with the lemon rind and juice (to prevent discolouration) and add to the salad with the diced beetroot.

2 Whisk all the ingredients for the dressing together; the mustard will make the dressing quite thick. Pour over the salad, toss and serve immediately.

new potatoes niçoise

A SALAD NIÇOISE USUALLY FEATURES TUNA, BUT I HAVE USED ANCHOVIES AND NEW POTATOES, FRESHLY COOKED AND STILL WARM IN THEIR SKINS. **SERVES 6 TO 8**

450 g (1 lb) small new potatoes, scrubbed

Salad greens

4 medium tomatoes, cut into wedges

100 g (3½ oz) cold cooked broad beans

4 hard-boiled eggs, quartered

2 tbsp chopped fresh mixed herbs

25 g (1 oz) small black olives

Salt and freshly ground black pepper

60-g (2-oz) tin anchovy fillets

2 tbsp butter

1 Bring the potatoes to the boil in a pan of water, then simmer for 10 to 12 minutes, or until just cooked.

2 Prepare the salad while the potatoes are cooking. Cover the bottom of a large bowl or platter with the salad greens, then arrange the tomatoes, broad beans and hard-boiled eggs around the edge. Sprinkle the salad with the herbs and olives, then season lightly with salt and pepper. Cut the anchovy fillets in half lengthwise and arrange the pieces over the salad, reserving the oil.

3 Drain the potatoes and return them to the pan. Add the butter, tossing the potatoes until it has melted, then arrange the potatoes in the centre of the salad. Add the oil from the anchovies to the butter left in the pan, stir in a few grinds of pepper, then pour the mixture over the salad and serve immediately.

spinach salad

THIS SALAD IS PACKED WITH TANGY FLAVOURS AND SHOULD BE SERVED THE MOMENT IT IS MADE. **SERVES 4**

40 g (1½ oz) pine kernels

4 handfuls young spinach leaves, washed and dried

2 handfuls rocket

125 g (4½ oz) cherry tomatoes, halved

Shavings of fresh Parmesan cheese

Salt and freshly ground black pepper

4 to 5 tbsp garlic vinaigrette

1 Heat a nonstick frying pan until evenly hot; add the pine kernels and cook until golden brown on both sides, shaking the pan almost continuously to stop the pine kernels from burning. Allow them to cool on kitchen paper.

2 Mix the spinach and rocket together in a large, flat dish, tearing the rocket into bite-sized pieces. Add the tomatoes and pine kernels, then add Parmesan cheese to taste; an easy way to cut the shavings is with a potato peeler.

3 Season the salad lightly with salt and pepper, then add the vinaigrette and toss before serving.

summer couscous salad

REMOVE THE PEPPER SKINS AFTER ROASTING BY PEELING FROM THE FLOWER END. **SERVES 6**

2 medium red peppers

3 to 4 small chillies

300 g (10½ oz) couscous

75 g (2¾ oz) pine kernels, toasted

100 g (3½ oz) finely sliced button
    mushrooms

1 small courgette, finely chopped

3 tbsp vinaigrette or extra-virgin
    olive oil

Salt and freshly ground black pepper

1 tbsp chopped fresh parsley

1 small avocado, sliced and tossed in
    lemon juice

1 Preheat the oven to 200°C/400°F/Gas 6. Place the red peppers and the chillies on a baking tray and roast in the oven for 20 to 40 minutes, turning once during cooking. The chillies may only take 20 minutes to blacken and should be removed as soon as they are ready. Cover the hot peppers with a damp teatowel and leave until cool. Peel, discard the core and seeds, and chop the flesh.

2 Cover the couscous with boiling water and allow it to stand for at least 20 minutes; add a little more water if it seems dry, but do not drown the grains. Drain well. Add the roasted peppers and all the remaining ingredients, except the avocado, and toss thoroughly. Transfer to a bowl or platter and garnish with the avocado just before serving.

lentil salad

LENTILS AND CURRY ARE ALWAYS A NATURALLY DELICIOUS COMBINATION. **SERVES 4 TO 6**

425-g (15-oz) tin green lentils,
    drained and rinsed

100 g (3 oz) grated carrot

2 sticks celery, finely chopped

50 g (1¾ oz) sultanas

1 tbsp chopped fresh coriander

DRESSING

3 tbsp sunflower oil

1 tbsp white wine vinegar

½ tsp curry powder

Salt and freshly ground black pepper

1 Combine all the salad ingredients in a bowl. Whisk together the oil and vinegar for the dressing, add the curry powder, then season to taste.

2 Pour the dressing into the bowl, toss the salad well, then chill lightly for about 30 minutes before serving.

rice and pistachio salad

THIS SALAD IS TOSSED IN A HONEY DRESSING. **SERVES 4 TO 6**

250 g (9 oz) wild and white rice mix

50 g (1¾ oz) raisins

50 g (1¾ oz) pistachios, shelled and unsalted

4 spring onions, trimmed and sliced

4 medium tomatoes, chopped

DRESSING

50 ml (1¾ fl oz) clear honey

1 tbsp cider vinegar

Grated rind and juice of 1 lemon

2 tbsp olive oil

Salt and freshly ground black pepper

1 tbsp chopped fresh chives

1 Bring both types of rice to the boil in plenty of water, then cover and simmer for 20 minutes. While the rice is cooking, whisk all the ingredients for the dressing together and season to taste. Drain the rice thoroughly, then add the dressing and toss it with the grains. Transfer the rice to a bowl and allow it to cool completely.

2 Add the remaining ingredients to the salad and stir them carefully into the rice. Season to taste with extra salt and pepper before serving.

flageolet and tuna salad

THIS RECIPE IS BASED ON ITALIAN ANTIPASTO. **SERVES 3 TO 4**

425-g (15-oz) tin flageolet beans, drained and rinsed

100-g (3½-oz) tin tuna, drained

1 small red onion, finely sliced

1 to 2 small cloves garlic, finely sliced

2 ripe medium tomatoes, seeded and chopped

1 tbsp capers

Salt and freshly ground black pepper

3 tbsp olive oil

1 tbsp chopped parsley

Lemon wedge, to serve

Small Cos lettuce leaves, optional

3 hard-boiled eggs, optional

1 Place the beans in a bowl. Flake the tuna and add it to the beans with the onion, garlic, tomatoes and capers. Stir in seasoning to taste, then moisten the salad with olive oil.

2 Sprinkle with chopped parsley and serve with a lemon wedge. You can also serve with Cos lettuce leaves and wedges of hard-boiled egg if desired.

mushroom and hazelnut pâté

A FLAVOURFUL VEGETARIAN PÂTÉ – SERVE WITH SALAD LEAVES. **SERVES 6 TO 8**

200 g (7 oz) hazelnuts, toasted and chopped

100 g (3½ oz) fresh wholewheat breadcrumbs, tightly packed

1 medium onion

2 plump cloves garlic

450 g (1 lb) mushrooms, trimmed

4 tbsp butter

Salt and freshly ground black pepper

2 tbsp soy sauce

1 large egg, beaten

2 thin rashers smoked back bacon (optional)

1 Preheat the oven to 180°C/350°F/Gas 4. Combine the hazelnuts with the breadcrumbs in a bowl. Finely chop the onion, garlic and mushrooms, best done in a food processor.

2 Melt the butter in a large frying pan, add the mushroom mixture and cook slowly for about 5 minutes, until the juices run from the mushrooms. Allow to cool slightly, then add to the hazelnut mixture with plenty of salt, pepper and the soy sauce. Blend together with the beaten egg.

3 Lightly grease a small loaf tin. Stretch the bacon with the back of a knife, then arrange it in the base of the tin. Spoon the hazelnut mixture into the tin and smooth the top. Cover with greased foil and place in a shallow roasting tin. Half-fill the roasting tin with hot water.

4 Bake in the preheated oven for 1 hour, then remove the pâté from the roasting tin and allow to cool. Chill the pâté overnight in the refrigerator, then loosen it with a knife and turn out onto a serving plate. Serve with salad greens.

wild-rice-stuffed mushrooms

ONE MUSHROOM PER PERSON MAKES AN AMPLE STARTER. **SERVES 4**

50 g (1¾ oz) wild rice

75 g (2¾ oz) finely chopped watercress

175 g (6 oz) low-fat cottage cheese

4 spring onions, trimmed and chopped

Salt and freshly ground black pepper

4 large field mushrooms, peeled

Olive oil

Paprika

4 slices freshly cooked whole-wheat toast

1 Bring the rice to the boil in a pan of water, then simmer for 30 to 40 minutes until tender. Drain thoroughly and allow to cool slightly.

2 Mix the rice with the chopped watercress, cottage cheese and spring onions; season to taste. Preheat grill. Remove the stems from the mushrooms and brush the shells lightly with oil. Heat for 3 to 4 minutes under the hot grill until almost cooked. Arrange the filling in the mushroom shells, and cook for a further 3 to 4 minutes, until the filling is set and hot. Sprinkle a little paprika over the mushrooms and serve immediately on hot, lightly buttered wholewheat toast.

tortilla wheels with pineapple salsa

THESE MINI TORTILLAS ARE GREAT STARTERS. **SERVES 6 TO 8**

FILLING

150 g (5½ oz) cream cheese

1 medium green chilli, seeded and finely chopped

2 tbsp chopped fresh coriander

4 medium tomatoes, seeded and finely chopped

4 spring onions, finely chopped

1 medium pepper, red or yellow, seeded and finely chopped

100 g (3½ oz) grated Cheddar cheese

Salt and freshly ground black pepper

8 flour tortillas

SALSA

1 tbsp black or brown mustard seeds

1 medium orange

4 thick slices pineapple, fresh or tinned

1 small red onion, finely chopped

1 small green chilli, seeded and finely chopped

2 small tomatoes, diced

1 Beat the cream cheese until smooth, then add all the other ingredients for the filling. Mix well and season to taste with salt and pepper. Divide the mixture among the tortillas, spreading evenly. Place each tortilla flat on top of another, making four stacks of two, then roll them up tightly. Cover in cling film and chill for at least 2 hours.

2 Prepare the salsa while the tortilla rolls are chilling. Heat a nonstick frying pan until evenly hot, then add the mustard seeds and cook for 1 to 2 minutes, until the seeds begin to pop. Allow to cool. Grate the rind from the orange, set aside. Peel the orange and chop the flesh. Mix the orange and rind with the mustard seeds and all the other ingredients, seasoning to taste with salt and pepper. Let the salsa stand until required.

3 Preheat the oven to 200°C/400°F/Gas 6. Unwrap tortillas and trim away the ends. Cut each roll into eight slices. Place flat on baking trays and bake in the hot oven for 15 to 20 minutes, until well-browned. Serve hot with the salsa.

apricot, almond and tomato salad

THIS SALAD PAIRS PERFECTLY WITH CURRIED VEGETABLE CASSEROLE
(SEE PAGE 118). **SERVES 4 TO 6**

100 g (3½ oz) blanched almonds

Salt

Cayenne pepper

Salad greens

4 ripe tomatoes, cut into wedges

200 g (7 oz) dried apricots, chopped

6 tbsp mustard vinaigrette

Parsley

1 Heat a frying pan, preferably nonstick, until evenly hot, then add the almonds. Cook over moderate heat until evenly browned on both sides (the almonds may be toasted if preferred). Dust some absorbent kitchen paper with salt and cayenne pepper, then add the hot almonds and toss until well-coated with the seasonings. Allow to cool, tossing from time to time.

2 Line a platter or bowl with some of the salad greens. Mix together the tomatoes, chopped apricots and devilled almonds, and the rest of the salad greens of your choice and arrange on the platter. Spoon on the mustard vinaigrette and garnish with a sprig of parsley.

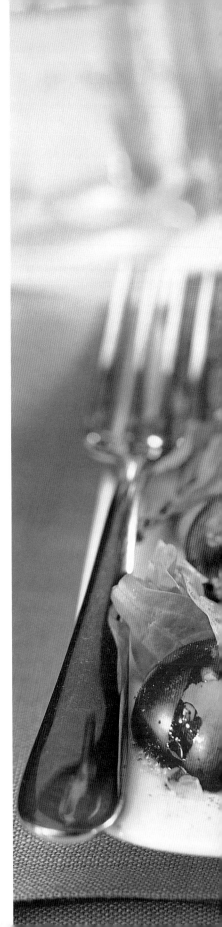

82　　**ABOVE** WARM JALAPEÑO BEAN DIP

brie quesadillas

THESE MEXICAN-STYLE SNACKS CAN BE EATEN AS EITHER A STARTER OR A LIGHT MEAL. **SERVES 6 TO 8**

Flour tortillas

FOR EACH TORTILLA

2 to 3 tbsp refried beans

40 g (1½ oz) ripe Brie, cut into slivers

Chopped avocado, pickled jalapeños and tomato salsa

1 Spread half of each tortilla with the refried beans, then top with the brie. Preheat a nonstick frying pan and add the tortilla. Shake over the heat until the cheese begins to melt.

2 Meanwhile, preheat the grill. Finish heating the tortilla through under the grill, until the cheese has melted and the beans are hot. If possible keep the uncovered tortilla away from the heat to prevent it from becoming crispy.

3 Top the cheese with avocado, jalapeño slices and tomato salsa, then fold the quesadilla in half to serve.

warm jalapeño bean dip

REFRIED BEANS – MASHED PINTO BEANS – ARE A STAPLE OF THE MEXICAN DIET. THEY ARE SERVED HERE ENLIVENED BY THE TANG OF CHILLI. **SERVES 8**

4 spring onions, finely chopped

1 small jalapeño chilli, seeded and finely chopped

1 medium clove garlic, crushed

1 tbsp olive oil

450 g (1 lb) refried beans

1 tbsp chopped coriander

2 small tomatoes, finely chopped

150 ml (¼ pt) soured cream

Salt

1 Cook the spring onions, chilli and garlic in the oil until softened but not browned. Add the refried beans and heat gently for 2 or 3 minutes before adding the coriander, tomatoes and soured cream.

2 Mix carefully and continue heating gently for a further 2 or 3 minutes. Season to taste with salt then serve immediately with tortilla chips, sliced vegetables or flat breads.

nut and cream cheese peppers

THESE ARE TASTY AND ATTRACTIVE STARTERS. **SERVES 4**

**150 g (5½ oz) mixed shelled unsalted
   nuts (peanuts, cashews, almonds
   and so on)**

Salt

Cayenne pepper

200 g (7 oz) low-fat cream cheese

1 clove garlic, crushed

Freshly ground black pepper

1 medium red pepper

1 medium green pepper

Wholewheat toast

1 Heat a nonstick frying pan over medium heat until hot, then add the nuts and cook until browned on all sides. Scatter salt and cayenne over some absorbent kitchen paper, add the hot nuts and toss in the seasonings. Chop the nuts roughly when cooled.

2 Beat the cream cheese until smooth, then add the garlic and nuts. Season to taste with extra salt, if necessary, and black pepper. Cut the tops from the peppers and remove the seeds and cores. Pack the filling into the peppers, pressing it down firmly with the back of a spoon.

3 Chill the peppers for 2 to 3 hours before slicing crosswise in 4. Serve one slice of each pepper to each person, with wholewheat toast.

roasted tomato tartlets

FOR AN EXTRA MEDITERRANEAN TASTE ADD A FEW OLIVES TO THE FILLING. **SERVES 6**

DOUGH

250 g (9 oz) fine wholewheat flour

40 g (1½ oz) sesame seeds

½ tsp salt

1 large egg, beaten

75 ml (2½ fl oz) olive oil

3 to 4 tbsp water

3 small onions, finely sliced

2 small cloves garlic, halved

3 tbsp fruity olive oil

3 to 4 sprigs fresh thyme

2 bay leaves

4 to 5 large tomatoes, sliced

Salt and freshly ground black pepper

1 Mix together the flour, sesame seeds and salt, then make a well in the centre. Add the egg and olive oil and mix to a soft dough, adding water as necessary. Divide the mixture into six and shape to line six 10-cm (4-in) individual tart tins – this is easiest to mould into shape with your fingers. Chill the tart shells for at least 30 minutes while preparing the filling.

2 Cook the onions and garlic in the olive oil with the thyme sprigs and bay leaves for 30 to 40 minutes, until well-softened and reduced. Season to taste with salt and pepper, then remove the herbs.

3 Preheat the oven to 220°C/425°F/Gas 7. Fill the tart shells with the onion mixture, then top with the tomatoes, overlapping the slices and brushing them lightly with olive oil. Season well with salt and pepper and bake in the preheated oven for 20 to 25 minutes, until the dough is crisp and the tomatoes are just starting to blacken. Serve hot or cold with a small leafy salad.

quick-bake calabrian pizzas

FULL OF SOUTHERN ITALIAN FLAVOURS, THESE PIZZAS ARE STRONG, TANGY, AND EXCITING. **SERVES 6**

DOUGH

300 g (10½ oz) wholewheat flour

1 tsp salt

1 package active dry yeast

1 tbsp olive oil

175 ml (6 fl oz) warm water

6 tsp tapenade

1 red onion, finely sliced

12 halves sun-dried tomatoes in oil, chopped

1 tbsp basil leaves, roughly torn

Salt and freshly ground black pepper

60-g (2-oz) tin anchovy fillets, chopped

125 g (4 oz) mozzarella cheese, sliced

1 Mix together the flour, salt and yeast in a bowl and make a well in the centre. Add the oil and most of the water, then mix to a soft but manageable dough, adding more water if necessary. Knead well until smooth and elastic.

2 Preheat the oven to 220°C/425°F/Gas 7. Divide the dough into six parts and roll out into circles 15 cm (6 in) in diameter. Fold the edges of the dough over to form a lip, then place the bases on lightly greased baking trays. Cover and leave in a warm place for 20 to 25 minutes, until the dough rises.

3 Spread each pizza base with one teaspoon of tapenade, arrange the onion over the bases and scatter with the chopped sun-dried tomatoes. Add the torn basil leaves with plenty of salt and pepper, and scatter the chopped anchovies over the pizzas. Arrange the mozzarella slices over the pizzas, then spoon the oil from the anchovies over the cheese.

4 Bake the pizzas in the preheated oven for 15 minutes, until the bases are crisp and the cheese has melted. Serve immediately.

ABOVE RATATOUILLE WITH MELON

spiced vegetables with yoghurt

THIS DISH CAN BE SERVED COLD, BUT I MUCH PREFER IT WARM. **SERVES 6**

600 g (1¼ lb) prepared vegetables (courgette, aubergine, pepper, cucumber, onions, mushrooms, etc.) sliced or matchsticks

2 plump cloves garlic, crushed

1 tsp cumin seeds

1 tbsp coriander seeds

3 green cardamoms, crushed and seeded

3 tbsp oil

225 g (8 oz) chickpeas, freshly cooked or tinned, drained

225 g (8 oz) thick plain yoghurt

Grated rind of 1 lemon

2 tbsp chopped fresh coriander

Salt and freshly ground black pepper

1 tbsp finely grated fresh ginger

1 Prepare the vegetables and mix with the crushed garlic. Heat a nonstick frying pan and add the cumin, coriander and cardamom seeds. Fry gently for 1 to 2 minutes until the seeds begin to pop, then transfer the spices to a mortar and pestle or a spice mill and grind – the ground spices may be sieved to remove excess coriander husks, if preferred.

2 Heat the oil in the spice pan, add the vegetables and cook for 4 to 5 minutes, until they begin to soften. Return the spices to the pan, add the chickpeas and continue cooking until the vegetables are tender and the beans are hot.

3 Mix the yoghurt with the lemon rind and chopped fresh coriander, then pour it over the vegetables in the pan. Mix gently, then add salt and pepper to taste before adding the grated ginger. Serve immediately, or let cool first.

ratatouille with melon

WATERMELON IS A GREAT ALTERNATIVE MELON FOR THIS DISH. **SERVES 8**

1 large onion, sliced

1 medium aubergine, sliced

4 tbsp olive oil

2 medium courgettes, thickly sliced

1 medium green pepper, diced

2 to 3 plump cloves garlic, finely sliced

Two 400 g (14 oz) tins chopped tomatoes

Salt and freshly ground black pepper

2 to 3 tbsp freshly torn basil leaves

175 g (6 oz) melon balls, either honeydew, cantaloupe or watermelon

1 Cook the onion and aubergine in the olive oil until the aubergine starts to brown, then add the courgettes, green pepper and garlic and cook for a further 5 minutes. Add the chopped tomatoes, salt and pepper and bring to the boil. Simmer for about 10 minutes, until the sauce has thickened but the vegetables still retain their texture.

2 Season the ratatouille to taste, then leave to cool. Add the basil and melon just before serving at room temperature.

(If you are preparing this dish to use in the recipe Ratatouille and Goat's Cheese Quiche, see page 111, do not add melon.)

aubergine pâté

THIS PÂTÉ OOZES MEDITERRANEAN PROMISE AND CAN DOUBLE AS A DIP. **SERVES 6 TO 8**

1 small onion, finely chopped

1 tbsp olive oil

1 medium aubergine, trimmed and
  thinly sliced

1 small clove garlic, crushed

125 ml (4 fl oz) tomato purée or thick
  tomato juice

1 tbsp fresh oregano

200 g (7 oz) low-fat cream cheese

Salt and freshly ground black pepper

1 Cook the onion in the oil until it starts to soften, then add the aubergine slices and cook, covered, for about 10 minutes until tender. Add the garlic and allow to cool.

2 Blend the aubergine mixture with all the remaining ingredients in a blender or food processor until almost smooth – the aubergine skin will keep the texture of the pâté slightly grainy. Season to taste, then chill for 30 minutes. The pâté should not be served too cold as this will impair the flavour – if it has been chilled overnight it should be allowed to stand at room temperature for about an hour before serving.

hummus

THIS MIDDLE EASTERN DIP IS DELICIOUS WITH FRESH BREAD OR CRUDITÉS. **SERVES 8**

150 g (5½ oz) chickpeas, soaked
  overnight or tinned

2 to 3 plump cloves garlic

100 g (3½ oz) tahini

100 ml (3 fl oz) olive oil

Salt and freshly ground black pepper

Juice of ½ lemon (optional)

Paprika

1 Rinse the chickpeas under cold running water, and bring them to the boil in a pan of fresh water and simmer for about 1½ hours, until tender. Leave to cool, then drain the beans, reserving some of the water. If using tinned, drain and reserve the liquid.

2 Place the chickpeas in a blender or food processor with the garlic, tahini and olive oil and blend until smooth. Add as much water from the beans as necessary to make a thick paste. Season well with salt and pepper, then add lemon juice to taste.

3 Spoon the hummus into a serving dish and chill lightly. Sprinkle with paprika just before serving with warm wholewheat pitta bread.

devilled leek crostini

SERVE WITH CRISP SALAD OR SOUP. **SERVES 4**

4 slices wholewheat bread

2 small leeks, finely sliced

2 plump cloves garlic, crushed

3 tbsp fruity olive oil

1 tsp dry mustard, or 2 tsp mustard

1 tsp cayenne pepper

**50 g (1¾ oz) freshly grated Parmesan
  cheese**

3 tbsp soured cream

1 Preheat the oven to 175°C/350°F/Gas 4. Bake the bread on a baking tray for 25 to 30 minutes, until dry and crisp. For extra flavour, brush the bread lightly with olive oil before baking.

2 Cook the leeks and garlic in the oil until they begin to soften, then add the mustard and cayenne. Continue cooking until the leeks are very soft. Add the cheese and cream, then season well with salt, pepper and extra cayenne as required.

3 Spread the leeks over the prepared toasts and cook under a hot grill for 2 to 3 minutes, until the leeks start to brown. Serve immediately.

ABOVE GUACAMOLE

stuffed anaheim chillies

DON'T PEEL THE CHILLIES – THE SKIN WILL COME OFF EASILY WHEN THEY ARE COOKED. **SERVES 4**

1 small onion, finely chopped

1 tbsp oil

1 tsp ground allspice

½ tsp chilli powder

100 g (3½ oz) red lentils

400 g (14 oz) tin chopped tomatoes

175 ml (3 fl oz) water or stock

½ tsp salt

4 large Anaheim chillies

100 g (3 oz) soft goat's cheese

1 Cook the onion in the oil until softened but not browned, then add the spices and cook slowly for another minute. Stir in the lentils, tomatoes and water and season with the salt. Bring to the boil and simmer for about 30 minutes, until the lentils are soft. Season to taste, adding extra salt if necessary.

2 Preheat the oven to 200°C/400°F/Gas 6. Cut the chillies in half lengthwise and remove the membranes and seeds. Place the shells in a roasting tin, then fill them with the lentil mixture and top with spoonfuls of the goat's cheese.

3 Bake the chillies in the preheated oven for 30 minutes until the cheese has melted and browned and the chillies are tender. Serve immediately.

guacamole

A TRUE GUACAMOLE SHOULD HAVE A SLIGHTLY ROUGH TEXTURE, NOT BE BLENDED TO A PASTE. **SERVES 4**

2 large ripe avocados

2 medium tomatoes, seeded and chopped

1 small mild green chilli, seeded and finely chopped

Grated rind and juice of 1 lime

2 spring onions, trimmed and finely chopped

1 to 2 medium cloves garlic, crushed

½ tsp salt

1 Scoop the flesh from the avocados and mash it roughly with a fork. Add all the remaining ingredients, seasoning gradually with the salt to taste.

2 Serve at room temperature or chilled with corn chips, tortilla chips or sliced vegetables.

stuffed courgettes with tomato sauce

BOAT-SHAPED COURGETTES ARE PERFECT FOR HOLDING STUFFINGS. **SERVES 4**

4 small courgettes, trimmed

1 large onion, finely chopped

100 g (3 oz) roughly chopped button
    mushrooms

2 small cloves garlic

2 tbsp oil

40 g (1½ oz) fresh wholewheat
    breadcrumbs

Salt and freshly ground black pepper

1 tbsp pine kernels

1 tbsp sunflower seeds

1 tbsp basil leaves, roughly torn

400 g (14 oz) tin chopped tomatoes

40 g (1½ oz) grated Cheddar cheese
    (optional)

1 Preheat the oven to 190°C/375°F/Gas 5. Cut each courgette in half lengthwise and scoop out the flesh with a teaspoon. Arrange the shells in a buttered ovenproof dish, chop the reserved flesh, and set to one side.

2 Finely chop half the onion, the mushrooms and one clove garlic in a food processor. Cook the mixture in one tablespoon of oil until the juices run from the mushrooms, then remove from the heat and mix in the breadcrumbs, seasonings and courgette flesh. Add the pine kernels and sunflower seeds, then stuff the mixture into the courgette shells and pack well.

3 Prepare the tomato sauce by cooking the remaining onion in the remaining oil until soft. Crush the remaining garlic and add it with the basil and tomatoes. Season well, then simmer for about 10 minutes, until reduced and thickened. Pour the sauce over the courgettes, sprinkle with the grated cheese if used and bake in the preheated oven for 20 to 25 minutes, until the courgettes are tender. Serve with a salad.

crab with ginger and grapefruit

I FIRST HAD THIS DISH IN A RESTAURANT IN SELSEY, ONE OF THE BEST CRAB-PRODUCING AREAS IN ENGLAND. IT IS WORTH SEEKING OUT FRESH CRABS FOR THIS DISH. **SERVES 2**

2 dressed crabs or 125 g (4 oz) crab
    meat

500 g (1¾ oz) fresh brown
    breadcrumbs

1 medium grapefruit

Salt and freshly ground black pepper

2.5-cm (1-in) piece ginger, grated

1 Scoop the crab meat from the shells into a bowl and set the shells aside. Mix the crab meat with the breadcrumbs. Grate the rind from the grapefruit, then add it to the crab with the chopped flesh of the fruit. Season well and add the ginger. Arrange the mixture in the shells and carefully clean the edges.

2 Preheat the grill, then grill the crabs under medium heat for 5 to 6 minutes until piping hot. Serve just as they are, or with a very small salad garnish.

crab balls with sweet lime sauce

USE TINNED OR FRESH CRABMEAT, WHICHEVER IS EASIER. **SERVES 4**

SAUCE

Grated rind and juice of 2 limes

1 tbsp Demerara sugar

1 small red chilli, seeded and very finely chopped

250-g (8-oz) tin white crab meat, drained and squeezed dry

75 g (2¾ oz) fresh wholewheat breadcrumbs

4 spring onions, trimmed and very finely chopped

Salt and freshly ground black pepper

Nutmeg, freshly grated

1 large egg, beaten

75 ml (3 fl oz) sunflower oil

1 Mix all the ingredients for the sauce together and set aside until needed.

2 Mix the crab meat with the breadcrumbs and spring onions then season with salt, pepper and nutmeg. Add the egg and blend the mixture together. Shape into 20 walnut-sized pieces – you may have to flour your hands to do this.

3 Heat the oil in a frying pan and add the crab balls. Fry them for 4 to 5 minutes until evenly browned all over, turning occasionally. Drain on absorbent kitchen paper, then serve immediately with the lime sauce for dipping.

3 Main dishes

A high-fibre diet based on grains and pulses may appear to be little different from a vegetarian eating pattern but not all high-fibre disciples have forsaken meat. I am a meat eater but, like so many other people, I now eat significantly less meat than I used to. By following a high-fibre diet and incorporating recipes that not only taste good but are also varied in style and texture, and filling, I do not miss the meat I used to eat.

Several of the dishes included here contain a mixture of meat or poultry and high-fibre foods. For example, in place of the classic Beef Bourguignon, which is often rich and heavy, I have included a Chicken and Butter Bean Bourguignon. The chicken contains less fat than beef and the beans mean that you need less chicken in each helping, creating a very healthy alternative to the classic beef recipe.

Some of these dishes contain pasta and it makes sense to use a wholewheat variety in a high-fibre diet. I have yet to find an acceptable commercial wholewheat pasta, so I have made my own pasta for these recipes. Providing that you use a fine wholewheat flour, the pasta is easy to make, but a bread flour will be too coarse and the bran will tear the dough. As none of the recipes rely on the pasta for all their fibre, a regular white pasta will not diminish the fibre content of the dish.

I have not included any recipes for baked potatoes in this book, but they are certainly a very useful high-fibre food. If you feel your main dish is short of the essential ingredient, then serve a baked potato with it and eat it with the skin. However, a baked potato without butter or soured cream is like a tomato without salt, so watch the calories.

LEFT APPLE RATATOUILLE WITH SPICED PORK (SEE PAGE 142)

corn mexicali

YOU WILL NEED A STRONG, SHARP KNIFE TO CUT THROUGH THE CORN. **SERVES 4**

4 large cobs of corn, husked

4 tbsp oil

1 medium onion, finely chopped

1 tsp mild chilli powder

1 tsp ground cumin

1 plump clove garlic, crushed

1 small green pepper, seeded and chopped

Two 400 g (14 oz) tins chopped tomatoes

Salt and freshly ground black pepper

2 tbsp chopped fresh coriander

Tortillas or corn chips

1 Cut the corn cobs into slices approximately 2.5 cm (1 in) thick. Heat two tablespoons of oil in a large frying pan, add the corn slices and cook quickly on both sides until they start to brown. Remove from the pan with a slotted spoon.

2 Heat the remaining oil in the frying pan; add the onion and cook until it starts to brown. Add the spices and cook for another minute over low heat. Stir in the garlic, pepper and tomatoes and bring to the boil. Return the corn to the pan and simmer for 30 minutes, turning the slices once.

3 Transfer the corn slices to a warmed serving dish. Cook the sauce to reduce and thicken, then season to taste. Add the coriander; pour the sauce over the corn and serve immediately with tortillas, Mexican rice, refried beans or corn chips.

chickpeas with sesame sauce

A STRONGLY AND UNUSUALLY FLAVOURED VEGETARIAN DISH, IDEAL FOR THE EXOTICALLY MINDED. **SERVES 4**

250 g (9 oz) chickpeas, soaked overnight, or tinned

2 large onions, finely sliced

2 tbsp fruity olive oil

2 tsp ground cumin

1 tsp ground allspice

1 red chilli, seeded and sliced

4 large cloves garlic, finely sliced

400 g (14 oz) tin chopped tomatoes

225 ml (8 fl oz) dry white wine

350 ml (12 fl oz) rich vegetable stock

Salt and freshly ground black pepper

40 g (1½ oz) sesame seeds, toasted

1 Tbsp tahini

1 Preheat the oven to 160°C/325°F/Gas 3. Cook the onions in the olive oil in a flameproof casserole dish until soft but not browned, add the cumin, allspice, chilli and garlic and continue cooking over low heat for 1 or 2 minutes. Drain and rinse the chickpeas under cold running water, then add them to the pot with the tomatoes, white wine and enough stock to just cover the chickpeas. Season well with salt and pepper, cover and cook in the preheated oven for 1½ hours.

2 Stir the toasted sesame seeds and tahini into the casserole and season to taste. Garnish with mint and lemon rind if you like before serving.

lentil and pumpkin lasagne

PUMPKIN AND LENTILS MAKE A SATISFYING ALTERNATIVE TO THE TRADITIONAL MEAT
FILLING FOR LASAGNE. **SERVES 6**

1 large onion, finely chopped

2 tbsp olive oil

1 medium courgette, diced

1 medium green pepper, seeded and
    diced

1 to 2 medium cloves garlic, crushed

450 g (1 lb) pumpkin purée, fresh or
    tinned

100 g (3½ oz) red lentils

400 g (14 oz) tin chopped tomatoes

700 ml (1¼ pts) rich vegetable stock

2 tbsp chopped fresh mixed herbs

Salt and freshly ground black pepper

Fresh wholewheat lasagne made with
    175 g (6 oz) wholewheat flour and
    1 large egg or 6 large wholewheat
    lasagne sheets

225 g (8 oz) ricotta cheese

350 ml (12 fl oz) soured cream

100 g (3½ oz) grated Cheddar
    cheese, loosely packed

1 Cook the onion in the oil until softened but not browned, then stir in the courgette and pepper and cook for another 2 minutes. Add the garlic, pumpkin purée, lentils and tomatoes and stir well. Add the stock, herbs and seasonings and bring the sauce to the boil. Simmer for 20 to 25 minutes, until the lentils are soft and the sauce has thickened.

2 Preheat the oven to 200°C/400°F/Gas 6. Prepare the pasta by mixing together the flour and egg, then process it through a pasta machine into six thin strips of lasagne. Bring a large pan of water to the boil and cook the lasagne quickly, two or three sheets at a time, for 1 to 2 minutes, until it floats to the top of the pot. Drain and set aside.

3 Place half the lentil mixture in the bottom of a suitable buttered ovenproof dish and top with half the pasta. Repeat the layers. Mix the ricotta and soured cream together and season with salt and pepper. Add half the cheese, spread the mixture over the lasagne and top with the remaining cheese.

4 Bake the lasagne in the preheated oven for 30 to 40 minutes, until the topping is set and brown.

vegetable tortillas with mixed bean salsa

DON'T OVERFILL EACH TORTILLA – THEY ARE BEST EATEN WITH YOUR FINGERS. **SERVES 4**

SALSA

425-g (15-oz) tin mixed beans, drained and rinsed

1 small red onion, finely chopped

2 small cloves garlic, finely chopped

100 g (3½ oz) diced cucumber

1 red chilli, seeded and finely chopped

1 medium avocado, chopped

1 tbsp orange juice

1 tbsp white wine vinegar

Salt and freshly ground black pepper

2 tbsp olive oil

600 g (1¼ lb) diced mixed vegetables (leeks, onions, celery, mushrooms, peppers, and so on)

1 tsp chilli powder

400 g (14 oz) tin chopped tomatoes

Salt and freshly ground black pepper

TO SERVE

12 flour tortillas, warmed

Grated Cheddar cheese

Soured cream

Chopped fresh coriander, to serve

1 Prepare the salsa by mixing all the ingredients together and leaving for up to 1 hour, to allow the flavours to blend.

2 Heat the oil in a large frying pan or wok; add all the prepared vegetables and stir-fry quickly for 2 to 3 minutes. Stir in the chilli powder and the tomatoes and cook for a further 5 minutes, until the vegetables are just softened. Season to taste.

3 Spread some of the vegetable mixture over a tortilla, then top it with grated cheese. Add some salsa and soured cream. Dust with chilli powder and sprinkle with coriander. Then roll up and eat.

brazil nut loaf

THIS MOIST, SPICY LOAF IS COMPLEMENTED PERFECTLY BY TANGY SALSA. **SERVES 6**

1 large onion

225 g (8 oz) mushrooms

2 plump cloves garlic

1 tbsp ground coriander

1 tsp ground ginger

2 tbsp oil

200-g (7-oz) tin chopped tomatoes

1 tbsp tomato purée

200 g (7 oz) brazil nuts, roughly chopped

100 g (3½ oz) fresh wholewheat breadcrumbs

Salt and freshly ground black pepper

1 large egg, beaten

SALSA

1 tbsp cumin seeds

½ cucumber, diced

2 medium tomatoes, diced

1 small mild red chilli, seeded and diced

4 spring onions, trimmed and finely sliced

2 large cloves garlic, finely chopped

Salt and freshly ground black pepper

2 tbsp white wine vinegar

1 Preheat the oven to 190°C/375°F/Gas 5 and lightly grease a large loaf tin. Chop the onion in a food processor; add the mushrooms and garlic and process until the whole mixture is a thick paste. Cook the paste with the spices in the oil for 4 to 5 minutes, until the juices run from the mushrooms. Add the tinned tomatoes and tomato purée and cook for a further 4 to 5 minutes, to reduce the tomato juice.

2 Transfer the mixture to a large bowl and add the chopped nuts and breadcrumbs. Season well with salt and pepper, then bind with the beaten egg. Spoon the mixture into the prepared tin, cover with lightly oiled foil and bake in the preheated oven for 1 hour, or until set. Remove the foil and cook for a further 10 to 15 minutes.

3 Meanwhile, prepare the salsa. Heat a nonstick frying pan, add the cumin seeds and roast for 1 to 2 minutes. Crush lightly in a mortar and pestle. Combine the cumin with the remaining ingredients and leave the salsa for about 1 hour. Stir before serving.

hazelnut and courgette pasta

WHOLEWHEAT PASTA IS EASY TO MAKE IF YOU USE FINE WHOLEWHEAT FLOUR – OR USE
PREPARED PASTA IF YOU PREFER. **SERVES 4**

2 tbsp butter

2 to 3 tbsp olive oil

**4 to 6 small green and yellow
courgettes, sliced diagonally**

2 to 3 plump cloves garlic, crushed

**100 g (3½ oz) hazelnuts, toasted and
roughly chopped**

**50 g (1¾ oz) freshly grated Parmesan
cheese**

Salt and freshly ground black pepper

PASTA

350 g (12 oz) wholewheat flour

2 medium eggs

**or use prepared wholewheat
tagliatelle or fettucine**

1 Heat the butter and oil together; add the courgette slices
and cook over medium-high heat until browned and
softened. This takes about 12 to 15 minutes. Add the garlic
and hazelnuts once the courgettes have started to soften.

2 Mix the flour with the eggs to make a firm pasta dough.
Knead thoroughly, then process through a pasta machine
and cut into tagliatelle. Bring a large pan of salted water to
the boil; add the pasta and boil quickly for 2 to 3 minutes,
until just tender. If using prepared pasta, cook as instructed on
the package.

3 Drain the pasta, shake briefly, then add to the courgette
mixture in the pan. Toss well, seasoning with salt and
pepper, then sprinkle over the Parmesan, which will melt over
the hot pasta. Serve immediately, while still hot.

pasta primavera

A CELEBRATION OF THE FIRST MONTHS OF SUMMER WITH ITS SMALL,
BRIGHT GREEN, FULL-FLAVOURED VEGETABLES. **SERVES 4**

100 g (3½ oz) sugar snaps or mange tout, trimmed

100 g (3½ oz) fine green beans, trimmed and halved

200 g (7 oz) asparagus, trimmed and chopped

125 g (4½ oz) shelled broad beans

1 small leek, trimmed and finely sliced

1 tbsp butter

250 ml (9 fl oz) double cream

1 to 2 tbsp chopped fresh parsley

225 g (8 oz) wholewheat pasta

1 Bring a large pan of salted water to the boil. Cook the peas, beans and asparagus individually, plunging them into iced water immediately to prevent overcooking. Cook the peas for 2 minutes; green beans for 1 minute; asparagus stalks for 3 minutes, then add the asparagus tips and cook for a further 2 minutes; and the broad beans for 3 minutes.

2 In a large pan, cook the leek slowly in the butter until soft but not brown, then add the cream and heat until almost boiling. Drain the vegetables and add them to the pan, then heat gently for 2 to 3 minutes until piping hot. Stir in the parsley.

3 Cook the pasta in a large pan of boiling salted water, drain and shake dry. Add the pasta to the vegetables, tossing it in the cream, and serve immediately.

spinach and walnut wholewheat quiche

WALNUTS GIVE A DELICIOUS CRUNCH TO THIS QUICHE. **SERVES 4 TO 6**

PASTRY

125 g (4½ oz) butter

225 g (8 oz) wholewheat flour

Pinch of salt

FILLING

450 g (1 lb) frozen or fresh chopped spinach

Salt and freshly ground black pepper

Nutmeg, freshly grated

75 g (2¾ oz) walnut pieces, chopped

125 g (4½ oz) blue cheese, crumbled (Stilton or Danish)

300 ml (½ pt) milk

2 large eggs

1 Preheat the oven to 200°C/400°F/Gas 6. Blend the butter with the flour and salt in a bowl until the mixture resembles fine breadcrumbs. Mix to a manageable dough with warm water, then roll out and use the pastry to line a 23-cm (9-in) loose-bottomed pie tin. Line with absorbent kitchen paper then fill with dry beans. Bake in the preheated oven for 20 minutes.

2 Cook the spinach gently in a covered pan until piping hot; shake from time to time to prevent it from burning. Squeeze the spinach dry, then season to taste with salt, pepper and nutmeg.

3 Remove the paper and beans from the pastry and fill with a layer of the spinach, then a layer of walnuts. Crumble the blue cheese over the top of the filling.

4 Beat the milk and eggs and season with salt and pepper. Pour the custard over the spinach filling, then sprinkle with nutmeg. Reduce the oven temperature to 190°C/375°F/Gas 5 and bake the quiche for 25 to 30 minutes, until set. Serve warm or cold.

ABOVE RATATOUILLE AND GOAT'S CHEESE QUICHE

ratatouille and goat's cheese quiche

I SOMETIMES ADD NUTS TO THE VEGETABLES TO GIVE EXTRA TEXTURE. **SERVES 4 TO 6**

PASTRY

75 g (2¾ oz) butter

125 g (4½ oz) wholewheat flour

Pinch of salt

400 g (14 oz) ratatouille (see p. 89)

1 tbsp basil leaves, roughly torn

100 g (3½ oz) soft goat's cheese

Salt and freshly ground black pepper

300 ml (½ pt) milk or milk and single cream, mixed

2 large eggs, beaten

1 Preheat the oven to 200°C/400°F/Gas 6. Prepare the pastry by blending the butter into the flour and salt until the mixture resembles fine breadcrumbs. Mix to a firm, manageable dough with warm water, then knead lightly on a floured surface and roll out to line a deep 18-cm (7-in) pie tin. Chill the pastry lightly for 10 to 15 minutes, then line the pastry case with kitchen paper and fill with dry beans. Bake for 15 minutes in the preheated oven.

2 Remove the paper and the beans and spread the ratatouille over the partly cooked pastry. Sprinkle the basil leaves and goat's cheese over and season with pepper. Beat together the milk, the eggs and some seasoning, then pour the mixture into the pastry over the vegetables and cheese. Return the quiche to the oven, reduce the heat to 190°C/375°F/Gas 5 and cook for a further 35 minutes or until set. This quiche is best served warm.

millet and vegetable gratin

THIS RICH GRATIN IS PERFECT FOR A WINTER'S EVENING. **SERVES 6**

300 g (10½ oz) millet, washed

1 large carrot, finely sliced

1 medium onion, finely sliced

8 rashers bacon, finely chopped

200 g (7 oz) sliced button mushrooms

425 ml (¾ pt) thick tomato juice

Salt and freshly ground black pepper

2 tbsp basil leaves, roughly torn

40 g (1½ oz) grated Cheddar cheese

1 Preheat the oven to 190°C/375°F/Gas 5. Add the millet to a large pan of boiling water and simmer for 20 minutes, then drain. Cook the carrot and the onion with the bacon until they start to soften, then add the sliced mushrooms. Cook for a further 5 minutes until all the vegetables are soft.

2 Add the tomato juice and the drained millet, season well with salt and pepper and add the basil. Transfer to a buttered, ovenproof dish and bake in the preheated oven for 40 minutes. Scatter the cheese over the millet and return the dish to the oven for a further 30 minutes. Serve hot with a spicy tomato sauce or chutney.

curried lentil soufflé

LENTILS ARE AN UNUSUAL BASE FOR A SOUFFLÉ, AND CURRY AN UNUSUAL FLAVOURING, BUT THE FINISHED DISH IS DELICIOUS. **SERVES 3**

125 g (4½ oz) red lentils

1 to 2 tsp curry powder

350 ml (12 fl oz) stock or water

2 tbsp butter

1 tbsp wholewheat flour

150 ml (¼ pt) milk

1 tbsp Dijon mustard

3 large eggs, separated

Salt and freshly ground black pepper

1 Preheat the oven to 175°C/350°F/Gas 4 and lightly grease a 15-cm (6-in) soufflé dish. Bring lentils, curry powder and water to the boil in a pan, and simmer for 10 to 15 minutes until lentils have softened and cooked to a thick purée. Beat smooth, then transfer to a bowl to cool slightly.

2 Melt the butter in the same pan and stir in the flour. Cook slowly for 1 minute, then gradually add the milk. Bring to the boil, stirring all the time, and cook until very thick. Add the mustard, egg yolks and lentils and blend well. Season lightly.

3 Whisk the egg whites until stiff, then fold them into the lentil mixture. Turn into the prepared dish. Bake in the preheated oven for 30 to 40 minutes, until set. Serve immediately.

bean and vegetable pasties

A TASTY VEGETARIAN ALTERNATIVE TO THE FAMOUS PIES FROM CORNWALL, SOUTHWEST ENGLAND. **SERVES 4**

50 g (1¾ oz) mung beans, soaked overnight

PASTRY

100 g (3½ oz) butter

175 g (6 oz) wholewheat flour

Pinch of salt

1 medium onion, finely chopped

125 g (4½ oz) finely diced mixed root vegetables

50 g (1¾ oz) grated or finely diced Cheddar cheese

Salt and freshly ground black pepper

1 tbsp chopped fresh mixed herbs (optional)

1 Drain the beans and rinse them thoroughly under cold running water. Bring to the boil in a pot of fresh water, simmer for 30 minutes until tender. Drain and set aside.

2 Preheat the oven to 200°C/400°F/Gas 6. Prepare the pastry by blending the butter into the flour and salt. Add warm water to give a firm but workable dough, then knead lightly on a floured surface. Divide the dough into four and roll out into 15-cm (6-in) diameter circles.

3 Mix the mung beans with the remaining ingredients and divide the mixture among the pastry circles. Dampen the edges with water, then draw the pastry together over the filling, pinching the edges together to seal them. Place the pasties on a lightly oiled baking tray. Cook in the preheated oven for 30 to 35 minutes, until the pastry is crisp. Serve hot or cold.

quick bean pot

TINNED BEANS TAKE HOURS OFF THE PREPARATION WITH NO LOSS OF FLAVOUR! **SERVES 6**

1 large onion, finely sliced

2 tbsp olive oil

125 g (4½ oz) sliced carrots

125 g (4½ oz) swede, finely diced

2 medium courgettes, sliced

Two 425-g (15-oz) tins beans with their juice, e.g. mixed beans and red kidney beans

2 tbsp fresh oregano, chopped

Salt and freshly ground black pepper

2 tbsp tomato purée

50 g (1¾ oz) grated Cheddar cheese

1 Cook the onion in the oil in a large flameproof casserole dish until softened but not browned, then add the carrot and swede and cook for 3 to 4 minutes. Stir in the courgette, beans and juice, the herbs, the seasonings, and the tomato purée. Bring to the boil, then simmer for 30 to 40 minutes, until the vegetables are tender and the juice is reduced to below the level of the beans.

2 Preheat the grill. Season the casserole to taste and sprinkle with the cheese. Cook under the grill until the cheese has melted and browned.

ABOVE SPICED BAKED BEANS

spinach and pancetta risotto

FOR A PERFECT RISOTTO, ALLOW THE STOCK TO BE ABSORBED AT EACH STEP. **SERVES 4**

1 large onion, finely sliced

3 tbsp olive oil

2 cloves garlic, crushed

300 g (10½ oz) risotto rice

1.25 l (2 pts) rich vegetable stock

5 slices pancetta or thick bacon

Salt and freshly ground black pepper

Nutmeg, freshly grated

350 g (12 oz) spinach, shredded
  coarsely

Parmesan cheese shavings to serve

1 Cook the onion in the oil until softened but not brown, then add the garlic and rice and cook over a low heat for a further 1 minute. Add one-third of the stock, then stir gently until it has been absorbed, then add half the remainder and simmer again. Stir-fry the pancetta in a dry non-stick frying pan until crispy and set aside.

2 Season the risotto well, then add the spinach with the remaining stock and cook until the spinach has wilted and the stock has almost been absorbed. Serve the risotto garnished with the pancetta and slivers of Parmesan.

spiced baked beans

THIS IS MY VERSION OF THE FAMED BOSTON BAKED BEANS. **SERVES 4**

300 g (10½ oz) black-eyed beans,
  soaked overnight, or tinned

1 large onion, finely chopped

2 tbsp oil

½ tsp chilli powder

½ tsp ground cumin

1 to 2 plump cloves garlic, sliced

1 green chilli, seeded and finely
  chopped

400 g (14 oz) tin chopped tomatoes

225 ml (8 fl oz) rich vegetable stock

Salt and freshly ground black pepper

1 thick pepperoni or garlic sausage,
  thickly sliced

1 tbsp wine vinegar

½ to 1 tbsp Demerara sugar

Chopped fresh parsley to garnish

1 Drain the beans and rinse thoroughly under cold running water; set aside. Cook the onion in the oil until soft, add the spices and cook slowly for another minute. Stir in the garlic, chilli and beans, then add the tomatoes and stock. Season lightly, bring to the boil and cover to simmer for 45 minutes.

2 Season to taste with extra salt and pepper, then add the sliced sausage to the beans. Cover and simmer for a further 15 minutes. Season with the vinegar and sugar, stirring well, before garnishing with parsley.

ABOVE HARICOT BEANS WITH BROCCOLI

haricot beans with broccoli

THE SECRET OF A PERFECT CASSEROLE IS A WELL-FLAVOURED STOCK. **SERVES 4**

300 g (10½ oz) haricot beans, soaked
    overnight, or canned

1 tbsp oil

1 large onion, finely sliced

1 leek, trimmed and finely sliced

200 g (7 oz) sliced button
    mushrooms

¼ tsp mace

25 g (1 oz) chopped fresh parsley

225 ml (8 fl oz) dry white wine

225 ml (8 fl oz) rich vegetable stock

Salt and freshly ground black pepper

½ small red pepper, finely chopped

125 g (4½ oz) small broccoli florets

2 tbsp soured cream

1 Preheat the oven to 170°C/350°F/Gas 4. Drain the beans and rinse them well under cold running water.

2 Heat the oil in a flameproof casserole; add the onion and leek and cook until soft, then stir in the mushrooms and cook for a further 2 to 3 minutes until they soften. Add the beans, mace, half the parsley, white wine and sufficient stock to just cover the beans. Season lightly with salt and pepper, then bring to the boil. Cover the casserole and cook in the preheated oven for 1½ hours, until the beans are tender.

3 Stir the beans; most of the liquid will have been absorbed but there should still be a little at the bottom of the pan. Add extra salt and pepper then stir in the red pepper and broccoli. Cover the pan and return it to the oven for a further 15 to 20 minutes until the broccoli is just tender. Stir in the soured cream and serve with steamed carrots or a tomato salad.

lentils and rice

THIS IS A FILLING DISH THAT CAN BE SERVED BY ITSELF OR WITH A GREEN SALAD. **SERVES 4 TO 6**

250 g (9 oz) brown rice

1 large onion, finely sliced

1 to 2 tbsp curry powder, according
    to taste

3 tbsp olive oil

250 g (9 oz) cooked or tinned lentils,
    drained

Salt and freshly ground black pepper

2 hard-boiled eggs, chopped

3 tbsp double cream (optional)

1 to 2 tbsp chopped fresh coriander

1 Place the rice in a large pan of water; bring to the boil and simmer for 30 minutes, or until the rice is just tender. Drain.

2 Cook the onion with the curry powder in the oil over low heat until the onion is soft, then stir in the cooked rice and lentils. Cook for 2 to 3 minutes until piping hot, then add the chopped eggs and the cream, if used. Cook for a further 1 to 2 minutes.

3 Season well, then stir in the coriander leaves and serve immediately.

curried vegetable casserole

A VEGETARIAN VERSION OF THE AFRICAN DISH, BOBOTIE. **SERVES 6**

2 medium onions, finely sliced

2 tbsp sunflower oil

1 tbsp medium curry powder

1 tsp turmeric

700 g (1½ lb) mixed diced root
    vegetables

2 tbsp white wine vinegar

1 tbsp dark brown sugar

1 tsp salt

½ tsp freshly ground black pepper

1 thick slice wholewheat bread

100 g (3½ oz) seedless raisins

3 tbsp fruit chutney

125 mL (4 fl oz) water

4 to 5 lime leaves (optional)

25 g (1 oz) flaked almonds

1 large egg, beaten

150 ml (¼ pt) milk

1 Preheat the oven to 175°C/350°F/Gas 4. Cook the onion in the oil until it begins to soften, then stir in the curry powder and the turmeric and cook for a further 1 to 2 minutes over low heat. Add the prepared root vegetables, vinegar, sugar, salt and pepper and cook gently over low heat until the vegetables begin to soften.

2 Soak the bread in water for 3 to 4 minutes, then drain it, squeeze it dry and add it to the vegetables. Stir in the raisins, chutney and water, then pack the mixture into a buttered ovenproof dish. Bury the lime leaves in the mixture and cover the dish with buttered foil. Bake in the preheated oven for 1½ hours. Reduce the oven temperature to 150°C/300°F/Gas 2.

3 Remove the foil from the dish and sprinkle the almonds over the vegetables. Beat the egg with the milk, adding extra milk if necessary to make 225 ml (8 fluid ounces). Pour it over the vegetables; bake for a further 30 minutes at the lower temperature, until the custard has set. Serve with mango chutney and a mixed salad.

glamorgan sausages

THE ORIGINAL WELSH SAUSAGES WERE MADE WITH A LOCAL CHEESE, NOW NO LONGER AVAILABLE. **SERVES 4**

150 g (5½ oz) leeks, trimmed and
    finely sliced

1 tbsp oil

250 g (9 oz) cold mashed potato

100 g (3½ oz) grated old Cheddar
    cheese

Salt and freshly ground black pepper

1 tsp Dijon mustard

1 tbsp freshly chopped parsley

75 g (2¾ oz) fresh wholewheat
    breadcrumbs

2 to 3 tbsp olive oil

1 Cook the leek in the oil until soft but not browned, then mix with all the remaining ingredients, except the oil, adding sufficient breadcrumbs to make a very stiff dough. Divide into eight then shape into sausages, flouring your hands to make it easy to handle the mixture.

2 Heat the oil in a frying pan; add the sausages and cook quickly for 6 to 8 minutes, turning carefully to brown on all sides. Serve with a spicy fruit chutney or relish.

cracked wheat pilau

VERY COARSE CRACKED WHEAT GIVES THE DISH A LIVELY, NUTTY TEXTURE. **SERVES 4**

1 large onion, sliced

1 medium leek, trimmed and sliced

2 tbsp olive oil

1 tsp ground cumin

1 tsp ground ginger

**1 to 2 plump cloves garlic, finely
sliced**

4 sticks celery, trimmed and sliced

**1 medium red pepper, seeded
and sliced**

125 g (4½ oz) baby corn, halved

225 g (8 oz) cracked wheat

400 g (14 oz) tin chopped tomatoes

700 ml (1¼ pts) water or stock

Salt and freshly ground black pepper

**125 g (4½ oz) mange tout, topped
and tailed**

**6 halves sun-dried tomatoes,
shredded**

1 Cook the onion and leek in the oil until softened but not browned, then add the spices and cook for 1 minute. Add the garlic, celery, pepper and corn, and cook briefly before stirring the cracked wheat into the pan.

2 Add the tomatoes, stock and seasonings, then simmer for 12 to 15 minutes, stirring occasionally. Add the snow peas and sun-dried tomatoes and cook for a further 4 to 5 minutes. Serve with a tossed green salad.

millet rissoles with yoghurt sauce

MILLET REPLACES THE TRADITIONAL MEAT IN THIS VEGETARIAN ALTERNATIVE. **SERVES 4**

125 g (4½ oz) raw millet

150 ml (¼ pt) milk or milk and stock, mixed

1 tbsp butter

1 heaped tbsp wholewheat flour

Salt and freshly ground black pepper

4 spring onions, finely chopped

1 to 2 tbsp freshly chopped dill

100 g (3½ oz) fresh wholewheat breadcrumbs

YOGHURT SAUCE

1 tsp cumin seeds

Grated rind and juice of 1 lemon

2 tbsp chopped fresh coriander

350 g (12 oz) plain yoghurt

Salt and freshly ground black pepper

FOR FRYING

2 eggs, beaten

75 g (2¾ oz) dry or toasted breadcrumbs

100 ml (3½ fl oz) oil

1 Add the millet to a large pan of boiling water and simmer for 20 minutes, until soft. Meanwhile, place the milk, butter and flour in a pan and bring to the boil, stirring constantly. Simmer the sauce for 1 to 2 minutes until thickened, then season to taste and pour into a large bowl. Drain the millet and add it to the sauce with the spring onions, dill and breadcrumbs. Mix together, and allow to cool.

2 Shape the mixture into 12 rounds or rissoles; coat your hands in flour and toss the rounds in the beaten eggs, then coat in the breadcrumbs. Repeat this process if necessary to get a good coating.

3 Prepare the yoghurt sauce. Toast the cumin seeds in a heavy-based frying pan for 1 to 2 minutes, then crush lightly in a mortar and pestle or with the end of a rolling pin. Mix the cumin with the other sauce ingredients and place in a small pot over a very low heat to warm gently.

4 Heat the oil in the heavy frying pan until hot, then add the rounds and cook for 10 to 12 minutes until well-browned. Serve with the yoghurt sauce.

wild rice casserole

THIS RECIPE HAILS FROM MINNESOTA, ONE OF THE PRINCIPAL WILD-RICE-GROWING AREAS OF THE USA. **SERVES 4**

1 tbsp butter

1 tbsp olive oil

1 medium onion, finely chopped

1 medium red pepper, chopped

150 g (5½ oz) chopped mushrooms

100 g (3½ oz) pecan nuts, chopped roughly

150 g (5½ oz) wild rice

700 ml (1¼ pts) rich chicken or vegetable stock

4–5 tbsp chopped fresh parsley

Salt and freshly ground black pepper

Chopped fresh parsley to garnish

1 Preheat the oven to 160°C/325°F/Gas 3. Heat the butter and oil together in a large flameproof casserole, add the onion and pepper and cook slowly for about 5 minutes. Stir in the mushrooms and pecans and continue cooking until the juices run from the mushrooms, then add the wild rice. Stir well, then pour in the stock.

2 Bring to the boil and add the parsley. Cover and bake in the preheated oven for 1¼ to 1½ hours, until the rice has absorbed practically all the stock. Season to taste, and serve with a green salad.

chestnut and cranberry casserole

SLIGHTLY SWEET AND SOUR, THIS DISH IS FULL OF BRIGHT COLOURS AND TEXTURES. **SERVES 6 TO 8**

1 large leek, trimmed and sliced

1 tbsp oil

450 g (1 lb) peeled chestnuts, fresh or frozen

1 medium red pepper, seeded and chopped

1 medium courgette, quartered and thickly sliced

4 sticks celery, chopped

50 g (1¾ oz) raisins

1 tbsp soy sauce

1 tbsp chopped fresh coriander

1 cinnamon stick, broken

425 ml (¾ pt) rich vegetable stock

225 g (8 oz) fresh or frozen cranberries

2 tbsp Demerara sugar

Soy sauce to taste

Chopped fresh coriander to garnish

1 Cook the leek in the oil until softened but not browned, then add the chestnuts and stir over the heat until defrosted, if frozen. Add the pepper, courgette and celery; stir-fry for 1 minute, then stir in all the remaining ingredients except the cranberries and sugar.

2 Bring the casserole to the boil, then simmer gently for 10 to 15 minutes. Add the cranberries; continue to cook for a further 10 minutes. Remove the cinnamon stick and add about two tablespoons of sugar. Stir in extra soy sauce to taste. Serve with boiled rice, topped with chopped fresh coriander.

peanut and bean sprout risotto

DRY-ROASTED JUMBO PEANUTS ADD A DELICIOUS CRUNCH TO THIS DISH. **SERVES 4**

250 g (9 oz) brown rice

1 large onion, finely sliced

2 tbsp olive oil

1 medium red pepper, seeded and sliced

150 g (5½ oz) sliced mushrooms

3 tbsp soy sauce

4 hard-boiled eggs

2 handfuls bean sprouts

100 g (3½ oz) unsalted dry-roasted jumbo peanuts

Salt and freshly ground black pepper

1 to 2 tbsp chopped fresh coriander

1 Bring the rice to the boil in a large pan of water, then simmer for 35 to 40 minutes, until tender. Drain well.

2 Cook the onion in the oil in a large frying pan until softened but not browned. Add the pepper and cook for 1 to 2 minutes before adding the rice and mushrooms. Season with the soy sauce and stir-fry for 3 to 4 minutes, until the mushrooms are cooked and the rice has heated through.

3 Chop three of the hard-boiled eggs and add them to the pan with the bean sprouts and peanuts. Season the risotto with salt and pepper if necessary, then continue cooking for a further 1 to 2 minutes before adding the coriander. Slice the remaining egg into quarters and use to garnish the risotto just before serving.

sweet and sour vegetable stir-fry

ALL THE STIR-FRIED VEGETABLES SHOULD BE CHOPPED TO THE SAME
RELATIVE SIZE FOR EVEN COOKING. **SERVES 4**

250 g (9 oz) brown rice

100 g (3½ oz) carrot matchsticks

1 small red onion, chopped

125 g (4½ oz) baby corn, halved

4 sticks celery, chopped

1 medium leek, trimmed and sliced

200 g (7 oz) shredded Chinese leaves

2 tbsp sunflower or peanut oil

SAUCE

150 ml (¼ pt) pineapple juice

1 tbsp Demerara sugar

50 ml (2 fl oz) white wine vinegar

50 ml (2 fl oz) tomato ketchup

Pinch of salt

Coriander leaves and soy sauce

1 Bring the rice to the boil in a large pan of water and simmer for
30 minutes or until tender.

2 Meanwhile, prepare all the vegetables. Heat the oil in a large
frying pan or wok, then add the carrots, onion, corn, celery
and leek and stir-fry for 4 to 5 minutes, until starting to soften
but still crisp. Blend the ingredients for the sauce together and add
to the pot with the Chinese leaves. Continue stir-frying for 2 to
3 minutes until the cabbage begins to wilt. Stir in the coriander at
the last moment.

3 Serve the stir-fry on a bed of the freshly cooked rice and spoon
the sauce over. Provide soy sauce separately when you serve, for
people to add if desired.

caramelized onion tart

THIS SAVOURY TART MAKES AN EXCELLENT LUNCH DISH.

SERVES 6 TO 8

700 g (1 lb 9 oz) sliced onions

3 tbsp olive oil

6 small cloves garlic, peeled and left whole

3 bay leaves

4 to 5 sprigs fresh thyme

Salt and freshly ground black pepper

BASE

40 g (1½ oz) toasted chopped hazelnuts or almonds

175 g (6 oz) wholewheat flour

½ tsp salt

1 egg, beaten

50 ml (2 fl oz) olive oil

1 Cook the onions in the olive oil until they start to brown, then add the garlic, herbs and seasonings. Cook slowly for at least 1 hour, until softened and lightly browned.

2 Meanwhile, make the base by blending the dry ingredients together, then binding them with the egg and olive oil. Work into a dough, then roll out to a rough circle about 25 cm (10 in) in diameter on a baking tray. Chill for at least 45 minutes.

3 Preheat the oven to 220°C/425°F/Gas 7. Removing the bay leaves, spread the onion mixture over the nut base. Grind some black pepper over the onions, drizzle a little extra olive oil on top and bake for 25 minutes, until the base is lightly browned. Cool slightly before serving.

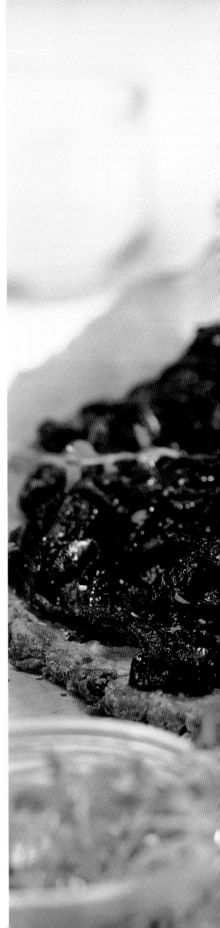

adzuki and fennel casserole

ADZUKI BEANS ARE VERY POPULAR IN CHINESE COOKING. I'VE COUPLED THEM HERE WITH THE
EXOTIC FLAVOURS OF THE PACIFIC RIM. **SERVES 6**

SALSA

1 medium orange

2 small tomatoes, chopped

½ small red onion or 4 spring onions,
  finely chopped

1 small green chilli, seeded and finely
  chopped

1 medium clove garlic, finely chopped

1 tbsp chopped fresh coriander

1 medium green pepper, seeded and
  chopped

Salt and freshly ground black pepper

175 g (6 oz) adzuki beans, soaked
  overnight and drained, or tinned

1 medium onion, finely chopped

1 large bulb fennel, finely sliced

1 tbsp oil

1 small red chilli, seeded and finely
  chopped

2.5-cm (1-in) piece root ginger,
  peeled and finely sliced

2 medium cloves garlic, finely sliced

1 tsp Chinese 5-Spice powder

1 cinnamon stick, broken

½ tsp ground cloves

1 piece lemon grass, very finely
  chopped

225 ml (8 fl oz) orange juice

400 g (14 oz) tin chopped tomatoes

250-g (8-oz) tin water chestnuts,
  drained and sliced

Soy sauce to taste

1 Prepare the salsa by grating the rind from the orange and chopping the flesh. Mix with the remaining ingredients and half the green pepper. Set aside.

2 Drain the beans and rinse under cold water. Cook the onion and fennel in the oil until soft but not browned, then add the chilli, root ginger, garlic, spices and lemon grass. Cook slowly for 1 to 2 minutes, stirring, then add the beans, orange juice and tomatoes. Bring to the boil, cover and simmer gently for 30 minutes.

3 Stir in the remaining chopped pepper and the water chestnuts and continue cooking for a further 10 to 15 minutes, until the beans are tender. Season to taste with soy sauce and serve with the salsa.

chicken and butter bean bourguignon

A HEALTHY APPROACH TO THE CLASSIC RICH DISH FROM BURGUNDY, FRANCE. **SERVES 4**

- **125 g (4½ oz) butter beans, soaked overnight**
- **1 tbsp olive oil**
- **1 tbsp butter**
- **4 large chicken thighs**
- **1 large onion, finely chopped**
- **2 rashers smoked back bacon, diced**
- **125 ml (4 fl oz) brandy**
- **2 cloves garlic, crushed**
- **4 sprigs fresh thyme**
- **2 bay leaves**
- **1 bouquet garni**
- **Salt and freshly ground black pepper**
- **1 tbsp tomato purée**
- **425 ml (¾ pt) full-bodied red wine**
- **100 g (3½ oz) sliced button mushrooms**
- **Chicken stock as needed or water**
- **Soured cream and chopped fresh chives to garnish**

1 Preheat the oven to 175°C/350°F/Gas 4. Rinse the beans thoroughly then bring to the boil in a pan of fresh water. Simmer until required.

2 Heat the oil and butter together in a flameproof casserole, then add the chicken thighs and cook quickly until browned all over. Remove the chicken with a slotted spoon; add the onion and bacon and cook until softened but not browned. Return the chicken to the casserole and remove the dish from heat. Warm the brandy gently until it ignites. Pour the brandy into the dish and leave until the flames subside, then return the dish to the heat and add the garlic, herbs and seasonings. Mix the tomato purée with the wine and pour into the dish, adding a little stock or water, if necessary, to cover the chicken. Bring to the boil, then cover the dish and cook in the preheated oven for 1½ hours.

3 Stir the mushrooms into the casserole; check the seasoning and that the beans are tender. Return the casserole to the oven for a further 15 to 20 minutes. Garnish with soured cream and chives.

chicken and kidney bean gumbo

A DELICIOUS HIGH-FIBRE VERSION OF THE FAMOUS SPECIALITY FROM
THE AMERICAN SOUTH. **SERVES 6**

1 large onion, finely sliced

3 sticks celery, sliced

2 tbsp olive oil

450 g (1 lb) okra, trimmed and sliced

2 large cloves garlic, finely sliced

400 g (14 oz) tin chopped tomatoes

2 tbsp butter

3 tbsp wholewheat flour

½ tsp chilli powder

1 tsp ground cumin

4 sprigs fresh thyme

Salt and freshly ground black pepper

750 ml (1½ pts) rich chicken or vegetable stock

175 g (6 oz) brown rice

225 g (8 oz) cooked chicken

400-g (14-oz) tin kidney beans, drained

100 g (3½ oz) prawns

Hot pepper sauce

1 Cook the onion and celery in the oil for about 5 minutes until starting to soften but not browned. Add the okra and garlic and cook for a further 3 minutes before adding the tomatoes. Cover the pan and simmer slowly for 15 minutes.

2 Prepare the sauce while the okra mixture is cooking. Melt the butter in a large flameproof casserole dish, then stir in the flour, spices, herbs and seasonings off the heat. Cook slowly for 2 to 3 minutes then gradually add the stock, again off the heat. Bring to the boil, stirring, then simmer for 2 minutes before adding the okra mixture. Season, return to the boil, then cover and simmer for 1 hour.

3 After 30 minutes, bring the rice to the boil in a pan of water, then simmer for 30 to 40 minutes, until tender. Add the chopped chicken and kidney beans to the gumbo. Return to the boil and simmer for 10 minutes, then add the prawns and cook for a further 5 minutes. Season to taste, adding pepper sauce as required, and serve garnished with spoonfuls of the cooked rice.

chicken and vegetable fricassee

THE CHICKEN MAY BE REPLACED BY COOKED BEANS IF PREFERRED. **SERVES 4**

1 tbsp oil

225 g (8 oz) cooked chicken, shredded

600 g (1¼ lb) prepared mixed vegetables, diced or sliced

125 ml (4 fl oz) dry white wine

225 ml (8 fl oz) soured cream

Salt and freshly ground black pepper

Chopped fresh parsley

1 Heat the oil in a frying pan; add the chicken and cook quickly until starting to brown, then add the prepared vegetables, tossing them in the hot juices. Cover the pan and cook slowly for about 8 to 10 minutes, until the vegetables have softened in the steam.

2 Pour the wine into the pan and cook quickly, stirring all the time, until the wine has reduced by half. Stir in the soured cream, season to taste, then heat gently without boiling. Serve with rice, garnished with chopped parsley.

cassoulet

THIS CLASSIC FRENCH DISH IS WELL WORTH THE LENGTHY BUT NOT DIFFICULT PREPARATION. **SERVES 8**

400 g (14 oz) haricot beans, soaked overnight

2 large onions, finely sliced

3 tbsp olive oil

2 cloves garlic, crushed

450 g (1 lb) diced cooked meats (such as chicken, ham, garlic sausage, goose, duck)

Salt and freshly ground black pepper

40 g (1½ oz) chopped fresh parsley

3 medium tomatoes, chopped

750 ml (1½ pts) rich chicken or vegetable stock

150 g (5½ oz) wholewheat breadcrumbs

1 Drain the beans and rinse them thoroughly under cold running water. Bring to the boil in a pot of fresh water, then cover and simmer for 1½ hours, until tender. Drain and keep until required.

2 Preheat the oven to 160°C/325°F/Gas 3. Cook the onions in the oil in a large flameproof casserole dish until lightly browned, then add the garlic. Remove from the heat and add the meats in a thick layer, seasoning with a little salt and pepper and about half the parsley. Layer the tomatoes on top of the meats, then cover with the cooked beans. Sprinkle with the remaining parsley and with plenty of seasoning, then add the stock, which should come to just below the level of the beans. Bring to the boil, cover and bake for 1½ hours.

3 Remove the lid. Make a thick layer of breadcrumbs over the cassoulet and return it to the oven for a further 20 to 30 minutes, uncovered, until the breadcrumbs have browned lightly. Serve immediately while still hot.

chicken and sweet potato curry

BLEND THE SAUCE INGREDIENTS TO A THICK PASTE BEFORE COOKING. **SERVES 4**

SAUCE

1 large onion

3 cloves garlic

1 green chilli, seeded and roughly chopped

2 tbsps tomato purée

1 tbsp mild curry powder

1 tbsp lime pickle or spiced fruit chutney

1 tsp Demerara sugar

1 tsp salt

2.5-cm (1-in) piece fresh root ginger, peeled and chopped

2 chicken breast fillets, skinned and diced

3 tbsps sunflower oil

250 g (9 oz) diced sweet potato

425 ml (¾ pt) water

Salt

3 tbsp fresh coriander leaves, torn

1 Purée all the ingredients for the sauce together in a food processor or blender until a thick paste forms. Cook the chicken in the oil in a large frying pan until it starts to brown, then add the sweet potato and cook until browned.

2 Spoon the curry paste into the frying pan and cook slowly for 2 to 3 minutes. Stir in the water. Simmer slowly for 20 to 25 minutes, until the chicken is tender. Add a little more water, if necessary, during cooking. Season to taste with salt, then add the coriander and serve.

chicken and flageolet bean risotto

ALWAYS USE ARBORIO RICE FOR RISOTTO TO GET THE MOIST, CREAMY TEXTURE THE DISH IS FAMED FOR. **SERVES 4**

125 g (4½ oz) flageolet or white kidney beans, soaked overnight or tinned

2 medium chicken breasts or 4 medium chicken thighs, skinned, boned and diced

1 tbsp olive oil

1 large onion, chopped

1 medium red pepper, seeded and chopped

2 plump cloves garlic, finely sliced

325 g (11½ oz) arborio rice, white or brown

1.25 ml (2 pts) rich chicken or vegetable stock

225 ml (8 fl oz) dry white wine

125 g (4½ oz) frozen or fresh peas

Salt and freshly ground black pepper

2 tbsp chopped fresh flat-leafed parsley

1 Drain the beans and rinse them thoroughly under cold running water. Place in a pan of fresh water, bring to the boil and cover to simmer for 1 to 1¼ hours, until tender.

2 Brown the chicken in the oil in a large frying pan, then add the onion and cook until soft but not browned. Stir in the pepper and garlic and cook for a further 2 minutes. Add the rice, toss it in the juices and cook for 1 minute. Add 450 ml (¾ pint) of stock and bring to the boil, stirring all the time, then simmer until the stock is absorbed, stirring occasionally. Add another 450 ml (¾ pint) of stock and cook until absorbed, then add the wine and repeat the process for a second time.

3 Stir the peas into the risotto with the remaining stock and cook, stirring constantly, until the stock is almost absorbed and the risotto is thick and creamy. Season to taste, and stir in the parsley just before serving.

spiced chicken with cabbage

A SATISFYING DISH THAT IS BEST SERVED WITH BOILED RICE. **SERVES 4**

1 medium onion, finely sliced

1 tbsp peanut oil

350 g (12 oz) shredded cooked
  chicken

½ tsp curry powder

1 small green chilli, seeded and finely
  chopped

2 cloves garlic, finely sliced

225 g (8 oz) green beans, cut into
  2.5-cm (1-in) lengths

225 g (8 oz) shredded white cabbage

1 to 2 tbsp peanut butter, according
  to taste

400 g (14 oz) tin chopped tomatoes

Salt and freshly ground black pepper

1 Cook the onion in the oil until it starts to brown, then add the chicken. Cook quickly for 2 or 3 minutes to heat the chicken through. Stir in the curry powder and cook slowly for 1 minute. Add the chilli, garlic and green beans and stir-fry for 1 to 2 minutes.

2 Next, add the shredded cabbage, peanut butter and tomatoes, then simmer for 6 to 8 minutes, until the cabbage just starts to soften. Season to taste with salt and freshly ground black pepper, then serve on a bed of boiled brown rice.

prawn chow mein

IF USING FROZEN PRAWNS, DEFROST THEM BEFORE USING FOR BEST RESULTS. **SERVES 4**

3 sheets thread egg noodles

1 large onion, chopped

2 tbsp sunflower or peanut oil

1 tsp Chinese 5-Spice powder

1 courgette, 1 carrot, 1 green pepper
  (seeded), cut in matchsticks

1 small red chilli, seeded and finely
  chopped (optional)

2 plump cloves garlic, finely sliced

200 g (7 oz) peeled prawns

2 large handfuls bean sprouts

50 ml (2 fl oz) sherry

50 ml (2 fl oz) soy sauce

100 ml (3½ fl oz) water

1 Soak the noodles in boiling water until needed, stirring them occasionally to separate the strands. Cook the onion in the oil in a large frying pan until softened but not browned. Stir in the 5-Spice powder and cook for a further 1 minute.

2 Add the courgette, carrot, pepper, chilli and garlic, and stir-fry for 3 to 4 minutes. Drain the noodles and add them to the frying pan with the prawns and bean sprouts. Mix the sherry, soy sauce and water together and pour the mixture into the pot. Cook for 2 to 3 minutes, tossing the vegetables and noodles together in the sauce. Serve piping hot, with extra soy sauce, if you like.

trout with wild rice stuffing

THE CRUMBLY RICE STUFFING GOES WELL WITH THE
DELICATE FISH. **SERVES 4**

STUFFING

1 small onion, finely chopped

1 stick celery, finely sliced

1 tbsp oil

½ small green pepper, finely chopped

1 small clove garlic, crushed

150 g (5½ oz) cooked wild rice (about 50 g (1¾ oz)

1 tbsp chopped fresh dill or parsley

Grated rind and juice of 1 lemon

Salt and freshly ground black pepper

4 trout, brown or rainbow

1 Preheat the oven to 200°C/400°F/Gas 6. Lightly butter a
suitable ovenproof dish.

2 In a frying pan cook the onion and celery in the oil until
softened but not browned. Add the pepper and continue
cooking until all the vegetables are tender. Remove the pan from
the heat and stir in the garlic and cooked rice. Add the herbs,
lemon rind and juice, then season to taste with salt and freshly
ground black pepper.

3 Clean the trout, removing the heads if preferred. Season the
cavities lightly and fill with the stuffing. Arrange the fish in
the prepared dish and cover with foil. Bake for 15 to 20 minutes,
according to the size of the fish, until just cooked. Serve
immediately while still hot.

stir-fried trout

THE ONLY WAY TO BETTER THIS IS TO USE FRESHLY-CAUGHT TROUT. **SERVES 2 TO 3**

3 tbsp oil

400 g (14 oz) mixed stir-fry vegetables

1 medium onion, cut into wedges

1 chilli, seeded and chopped

2 large trout fillets, about 450 g (1 lb), skinned and cut into 5-cm (2-in) pieces

200-g (7-oz) tin water chestnuts, drained and halved

2 handfuls bean sprouts

2 tbsp soy sauce

1 tbsp chilli sauce

1 Heat the oil in a wok or a large frying pan until almost smoking. Add the prepared vegetables, onion and chilli, and stir-fry for 1 minute.

2 Add the trout and water chestnuts, and continue cooking over very high heat for 2 to 3 minutes, until the fish is almost cooked – don't stir too vigorously or the fish will break up. Finally, add the bean sprouts, soy and chilli sauces and cook for a further 1 minute. Serve immediately over brown rice or noodles.

spanish-style haddock

SERVE WITH CRUSTY WHOLEWHEAT BREAD FOR A SUMMER LUNCH OR LIGHT SUPPER. **SERVES 4**

450 g (1 lb) thick haddock fillet or similar white fish, skinned

3 tbsp fruity olive oil

1 small mild onion, finely sliced

2 plump cloves garlic, finely sliced

100 g (3½ oz) sliced mushrooms

1 small red pepper, seeded and sliced

1 small green pepper, seeded and sliced

Salt and freshly ground black pepper

125 ml (4 fl oz) white wine vinegar

100 ml (3½ fl oz) water

1 tbsp sugar

1 Cut the fish into bite-sized pieces. Heat two tablespoons of the oil in a frying pan and fry the fish until just cooked. Transfer it to a glass dish. Heat the remaining oil in the frying pan; add the onion and garlic and cook until soft but not browned. Stir in the mushrooms and peppers and cook for a further 1 to 2 minutes – the vegetables should retain a crisp texture. Spoon the vegetables over the fish and season lightly.

2 Pour the vinegar and water into the frying pan and bring to the boil. Stir in the sugar until dissolved, then pour the liquid over the fish and vegetables. Leave to cool, then cover and place in the refrigerator for 24 hours.

lamb with lentils and prunes

RELISH THE CLASSIC FLAVOURS OF SOUTH-WEST FRANCE IN THIS TASTY CASSEROLE. **SERVES 4**

1 tbsp olive oil

1 tbsp butter

4 lamb chops or 450 g (1 lb) lamb fillet, cut into 4 pieces

1 large onion, sliced

3 sticks celery, sliced

2 large carrots, sliced

2 plump cloves garlic, finely sliced

1 tbsp wholewheat flour

425 ml (¾ pt) rich vegetable or lamb stock

200 g (7 oz) dried prunes

100 g (3½ oz) green lentils

6 juniper berries, lightly crushed

4 to 5 sprigs fresh thyme

Salt and freshly ground black pepper

1 Preheat the oven to160°C/325°F/Gas 3. Heat the oil and butter in a flameproof casserole dish and brown the lamb on all sides. Remove the meat with a slotted spoon and set aside until needed. Add the onion to the casserole and cook slowly until softened but not browned, then add the celery, carrot and garlic and continue cooking for a further 2 to 3 minutes.

2 Stir the flour into the vegetables and cook for 1 to 2 minutes, then gradually add the stock, stirring to scrape any sediment from the bottom of the dish. Bring to the boil; add the prunes and lentils and simmer for 2 to 3 minutes. Return the lamb to the casserole and add the remaining seasonings. Cover and cook in the preheated oven for 1½ to 2 hours. Season to taste before serving.

apple ratatouille with spiced pork

CIDER, APPLE AND CORN COMPLEMENT THE PORK
WELL. **SERVES 4**

MARINADE

3 tbsp black bean or hoisin sauce

2 tsp Thai 7-Spice seasoning

2 tbsp soy sauce

375 g (12 oz) pork fillet or tenderloin, in one thick piece if possible

100 g (3½ oz) black beans soaked overnight, or tinned

1 large onion, finely sliced

3 tbsp oil

2 to 3 plump cloves garlic, finely sliced

1 small aubergine, sliced

1 small green pepper, seeded and sliced

125 g (4½ oz) baby corn cobs, halved

400 g (14 oz) tin chopped tomatoes

1 large cooking apple, peeled, cored and sliced

225 ml (8 fl oz) dry cider or apple juice

Chives to garnish

1 Mix together the ingredients for the marinade, then add the pork and coat thoroughly with the mixture. Leave to stand for at least 1 hour, turning the pork once or twice.

2 Drain the beans and rinse them thoroughly under cold running water. Bring to the boil in a pan of fresh water, then cover and simmer gently until required.

3 Preheat the oven to 200°C/400°F/Gas 6. Transfer the pork to a small roasting tin and spoon the marinade over. Roast in the oven for 30 minutes. Cook the onion in the oil in a large pan until softened but not browned, then add the remaining ratatouille vegetables, the apple and the cider. Drain the beans, add them to the pan, then bring to the boil. Simmer for 20 minutes, until the beans and vegetables are tender. Slice the pork thinly and serve it with the ratatouille and baked or mashed potatoes, topped with chives.

spiced lamb with chickpeas

A SPICY STEW, RICH WITH MIDDLE EASTERN FLAVOURS. **SERVES 6**

75 g (2¾ oz) chickpeas, soaked overnight or tinned

250 g (8 oz) lamb, sliced

3 tbsp olive oil

1 medium onion, finely sliced

1 small aubergine, finely sliced

2 tsp ground cumin

1 tsp ground allspice

1 cinnamon stick, broken

150 ml (¼ pt) red wine

400 g (14 oz) tin chopped tomatoes

225 ml (8 fl oz) rich vegetable or lamb stock

100 g (3½ oz) dried apricots

Salt and freshly ground black pepper

300 g (2½ oz) couscous

75 g (2¾ oz) pistachios, unsalted

Olive oil

Chopped fresh parsley

1 Drain the chickpeas and rinse thoroughly. Bring to the boil in a pan of fresh water, cover and simmer for 30 to 40 minutes.

2 Fry the lamb in the oil in a pan until browned on all sides, then remove from the pan with a slotted spoon and set aside. Add the onion and aubergine to the oil and cook over high heat until golden brown, adding a little extra oil if necessary. Stir in the spices and continue cooking over very low heat for 1 to 2 minutes.

3 Return the lamb to the pan and add the wine. Bring to the boil and simmer until well reduced, scraping the bottom of the pan. Stir in the tomatoes, stock, apricots and seasoning. Add the drained beans, cover and simmer for 30 minutes.

4 After 20 minutes, pour a little warm water over the couscous and leave for 10 minutes. Transfer to a steamer tier. Stir the nuts into the stew; place the couscous over the pan, cover and cook 15 to 20 minutes. Dress the couscous with olive oil and season. Season the stew and serve on a bed of couscous. Garnish with parsley.

thai-style beef

USE RICE OR NOODLES INSTEAD OF POTATOES IF YOU
PREFER. **SERVES 4**

450 g (1 lb) small new potatoes in their skins

3 tbsp corn oil

8 thin slices topside of beef, cut into strips

200 g (7 oz) broccoli florets and stalks, roughly chopped

6 large spring onions, chopped

250 g (9 oz) sliced mushrooms

1 piece lemon grass, trimmed and sliced

2 medium cloves garlic, finely sliced

100 g (3½ oz) salted cashew nuts

100 ml (3½ fl oz) oyster sauce

50 ml (2 fl oz) water

3–4 tbsp chopped fresh coriander

1 Bring the potatoes to the boil in a pot of water, then simmer for 10 minutes. Drain and leave until cool enough to handle, then slice in half lengthways.

2 Heat the oil in a large wok or frying pan, then add the beef and stir-fry for 1 minute. Add the prepared vegetables with the lemon grass and garlic, and continue cooking for a further 3 to 4 minutes. Stir the potatoes into the pan with the cashews, oyster sauce and water, then cook for a further 1 to 2 minutes until the sauce is bubbling. Add the coriander immediately before serving.

4 Desserts

When time allows, dessert is the perfect ending to a good meal, a treat to be thoroughly enjoyed. Many of the desserts included here contain fruit. Berries and exotic fruits, such as mangoes, are best eaten in a simple fruit salad, especially if they are fully ripened, but using just a few fruits rather than filling a bowl with numerous varieties can produce a stylish, light dessert; for example, strawberries served with melon and orange. Make a change by serving a flavoured, blended cream instead of whipped cream – lime mascarpone is perfect with a dish of peaches and raspberries, for example.

Raspberries and blackberries are expensive to buy, even when they are in season, as they are time consuming to pick and have a very short shelf life. I usually buy them frozen in fruit mixes; then they are reasonably priced and make a wonderful base for any number of desserts.

Beans are not usually the first choice of ingredients for a dessert, but adzuki beans, which are semi-sweet, are good in both savoury and sweet dishes. The Sweet Bean and Apple Crumble that I have included here is delicious and I thoroughly recommend it. Although white rice does not contain as much fibre as brown, it is still a source of fibre and should not be disregarded in a high-fibre diet. I am a rice pudding addict and have included an everyday rice pudding, as well as a much creamier pudding with fresh mangoes and grapes stirred into it.

LEFT SUMMER FRUIT UPSIDE-DOWN TRIFLE (SEE PAGE 170)

plum and apple pudding

IN COLD WEATHER YOU CAN'T BEAT A WARM
SPONGE PUDDING. **SERVES 4 TO 6**

900 g (2 lb) ripe plums and cooking apples, mixed
100 g (3½ oz) light muscavado sugar

TOPPING
100 g (3½ oz) margarine
100 g (3½ oz) light muscavado sugar
1 large egg, beaten
225 g (8 oz) wholewheat flour
1 tsp baking powder
Pinch of salt
1 tsp ground ginger
1 tbsp milk

1 Preheat the oven to 190°C/375°F/Gas 5. Peel, core and slice the
apples, then cut the plums in half and remove the stones. Cut
the plums into quarters if they are very firm. Mix the fruits and
place in a suitable ovenproof dish – I use a 20-cm (8-in), round flan
dish – then sprinkle the sugar on top.

2 Cream the margarine and sugar for the topping until pale and
creamy, then beat in the egg. Mix the flour, baking powder,
salt and ginger, then fold into the egg mixture with the milk.
Spoon the mixture as evenly as possible over the fruit. Bake in the
preheated oven for about 30 to 35 minutes, until the pudding is set
and shrinking slightly from the sides of the dish. Serve hot.

banana bran custard

QUICK TO MAKE, THIS DESSERT WILL KEEP, REFRIGERATED, FOR UP TO 2 DAYS. **SERVES 4**

2 medium bananas, sliced

Grated rind and juice of 1 lemon

150 ml (¼ pt) soured cream or yoghurt

40 g (1½ oz) pecans, chopped

1 tbsp honey

25 g (1 oz) wheat or oat bran

Milk

1 In a bowl, toss the banana slices in lemon juice, then carefully mix in the cream or yoghurt, nuts, honey and bran. If the mixture is very thick, add one to two tablespoons of milk to thin it down.

2 Decorate with the lemon rind just before serving. If serving immediately, the honey may be drizzled over the cream in a zigzag pattern.

rum and raisin yoghurt ice cream

THIS MAKES A FULL-BODIED, BUT NOT TOO RICH, DELICIOUS DESSERT. **SERVES 6 TO 8**

125 g (4½ oz) seedless raisins

50 ml (2 fl oz) rum

2 large egg whites

75 g (2¾ oz) light muscavado sugar

75 ml (3 fl oz) water

150 ml (¼ pt) thick plain yoghurt

300 ml (½ pt) whipping cream

1 Soak the raisins in the rum for 20 minutes before beginning the ice cream.

2 Whisk the egg whites until stiff. At the same time, heat the sugar with the water until the sugar has dissolved, then bring the syrup to the boil and boil rapidly for 3 minutes. Beating continuously, pour the sugar syrup in a steady stream onto the whisked egg whites; continue beating for about 1 minute. Add the yoghurt and continue beating until the mixture is cool; this is best done in a mixer.

3 Whisk the whipping cream until thick and floppy but not stiff. Drain the rum from the raisins and into the yoghurt mixture; add the cream, and, finally, fold in the raisins. Turn the mixture into a bombe mould or a suitable container and freeze for about 4 hours, until firm. Remove from the freezer 20 minutes before required, to let it soften.

brown bread ice cream

THIS POPULAR VICTORIAN DESSERT HAS RECENTLY ENJOYED A GREAT REVIVAL. **SERVES 6 TO 8**

425 ml (¾ pt) milk

1 vanilla pod

4 egg yolks

75 g (2¾ oz) light muscavado sugar

150 ml (¼ pt) whipping cream

75 g (2¾ oz) wholewheat breadcrumbs, evenly toasted

1 Heat the milk with the vanilla pod until almost boiling, then leave to stand for 10 minutes before removing the vanilla. Beat the egg yolks with the sugar until a thick paste. Return the milk to the heat and bring almost to simmering point, then pour onto the egg yolks in a steady stream, beating all the time. Rinse the pan, return the custard to it and heat gently, stirring until the mixture coats the back of a wooden spoon. Do not be tempted to overcook the custard or it will curdle. Pour the custard into a bowl and allow to cool completely.

2 Chill the custard in a freezer for 1½ hours, until thick and slushy. Whip the cream until soft and floppy. Fold it into the custard with the breadcrumbs, then return the ice cream to the freezer. Stir after 1 hour, then leave for a further 2 to 3 hours until completely set.

3 Remove the ice cream from the freezer about 30 minutes before serving, to allow it to soften.

apricot bread and butter pudding

TUCK THE FRUIT INTO THE PUDDING SO THAT IT WON'T BURN
DURING COOKING. **SERVES 4**

3 to 4 slices wholewheat bread

Margarine or butter

100 g (3½ oz) roughly chopped dried apricots

50 g (1¾ oz) sultanas

425 ml (¾ pt) milk

3 large eggs

1 tbsp light muscavado sugar

1 tbsp yoghurt

Demerara sugar, to top

Cinnamon, to top

1 Preheat the oven to 175°C/350°F/Gas 5. Butter the bread and cut it into triangular quarters. Arrange half the bread in the bottom of a large pie dish. Scatter the dried fruits over, then top with the remaining bread. Beat the milk with the eggs and sugar, then pour over the pudding – if you leave the crusts on the bread, I suggest leaving the pudding to stand for 15 to 20 minutes before cooking, to allow the crusts to soften.

2 Bake the pudding for 35 to 40 minutes, until the custard is set. Serve warm, not hot, with a dollop of yoghurt and dusted with demerara sugar and cinnamon.

apricot cheesecake

ALWAYS USE GELATINE WITHIN SIX MONTHS OF PURCHASE. **SERVES 8 TO 10**

BASE

50 g (1¾ oz) butter

50 g (1¾ oz) honey

225 g (8 oz) muesli

350 g (12 oz) dried apricots, soaked in 350 ml (12 fl oz) water for 4 hours

200 g (7 oz) low-fat cream cheese, or strained cottage cheese

225 g (8 oz) thick plain yoghurt

1 tbsp powdered gelatine

2 large egg whites

Fine strips of orange rind

1 Melt the butter in a pan, then mix well with the honey and muesli. Press and smooth the mixture into the base of a deep, 20-cm (8-in), springform or loose-bottomed cake tin. Chill until required.

2 Reserve 75 ml (3 fluid ounces) of liquid from the apricots. Purée the fruit with the remaining juice in a blender or food processor until smooth – add a little extra water if necessary to achieve a smooth paste. Turn into a bowl and beat in the cheese and yoghurt.

3 Heat the reserved apricot juice until almost boiling in a small pan, then remove from the heat and sprinkle the gelatine over. Stir until almost dissolved then leave to stand for 2 minutes, until completely dissolved. Stir one heaped tablespoon of the apricot mixture into the gelatine – this helps to incorporate it evenly – then fold the gelatine into the apricot mixture. Whisk the egg whites until stiff, and fold them into the apricots.

4 Pour the mixture over the muesli base and smooth the top. Chill in the refrigerator for 2 to 3 hours until set. Carefully remove the cheesecake from the cake tin and decorate with strips of orange rind just before serving.

prune and walnut tart

BAKED IN CRISP PASTRY, THIS CREAMY TART IS GREAT FOR A SPECIAL OCCASION. **SERVES 6**

PASTRY

100 g (3½ oz) butter

225 g (8 oz) wholewheat flour

1 tbsp light muscavado sugar

1 large egg, beaten

FILLING

2 tbsp plum jam or apple jelly

150 g (5½ oz) stoned prunes, chopped

40 g (1½ oz) walnut pieces, chopped

300 ml (½ pt) milk or single cream

2 large eggs, beaten

1 tsp caster sugar (optional)

Freshly grated nutmeg

1 Prepare the pastry by blending the butter into the flour and sugar. Bind with the beaten egg, then knead gently on a lightly floured surface. Cover the pastry with clingfilm and chill in a refrigerator for 30 minutes.

2 Preheat the oven to 200°C/400°F/Gas 6. Roll out the pastry to line a deep 20-cm (8-in) flan or cake tin, preferably with a loose base. Line the pastry case with baking parchment and dry beans, then bake for 15 minutes. Remove the beans and parchment, and continue cooking for a further 5 minutes, until the base is dry.

3 Reduce the oven heat to 175°C/350°/Gas 4. Spread the jam over the base of the flan and top with the prunes and walnuts. Beat the milk or cream with the eggs and sugar, if used, and pour the custard into the flan and sprinkle with nutmeg. Bake for 40 minutes, or until lightly set. Serve warm or cold.

gooseberry and orange fool

THE PAIRING OF GOOSEBERRY AND ORANGE IS OUTSTANDING. **SERVES 4**

450 g (1 lb) gooseberries, topped

Grated rind and juice of 2 medium oranges

100 g (3½ oz) Demerara sugar

225 ml (8 fl oz) Devon cream

225 ml (8 fl oz) thick plain yoghurt

1 tbsp Demerara sugar

1 tbsp wheat or oat bran

1 Simmer the gooseberries with the orange rind, juice and sugar until just soft. Allow the fruit to cool, then fold it into the cream. Blend in the yoghurt, either mixing it completely or leaving it marbled through the cream mixture. Spoon into a glass serving bowl or individual dishes and chill for 1 hour.

2 Mix the remaining tablespoon of sugar with the bran and scatter over the trifle before serving.

baked bananas with rum

THE NATURAL SWEETNESS OF RAISINS AND COCONUT MEANS NO ADDED SUGAR! **SERVES 4**

4 large ripe bananas

125 mL (4 fl oz) orange juice

2 tbsp rum

40 g (1½ oz) seedless raisins

40 g (1½ oz) dried coconut

Vanilla ice cream

1 Preheat the oven to 190°C/375°F/Gas 5. Peel the bananas, cut them in half lengthways, then place in a suitable ovenproof dish that is just large enough for them. Mix the orange juice and rum and pour over the bananas. Sprinkle with the raisins and coconut.

2 Bake in the preheated oven for 15 minutes, or until the bananas are soft. Serve immediately with the ice cream.

mango yoghurt brulée

A DELICIOUS VARIATION ON CRÈME BRULÉE. **SERVES 4**

1 large ripe mango

350 g (12 oz) thick plain yoghurt

3 tbsp All-Bran® cereal, crushed

100 g (3½ oz) Demerara sugar

1 Peel the mango, remove the stone and chop the flesh, then divide it among four ovenproof ramekin dishes.

2 Preheat the grill. Blend the yoghurt with the cereal, breaking the strands into smaller pieces, then spoon it over the fruit. Spoon a thick layer of sugar over the yoghurt, so that it is covered.

3 Cook the puddings under the hot grill for 1 to 2 minutes, until the sugar has melted. Do not overcook, or the yoghurt will bubble up through the sugar. Allow to cool, then chill for at least 1 hour before serving.

date and ginger pudding

ON A TOTALLY DECADENT DAY, SERVE WITH TOFFEE OR BUTTERSCOTCH SAUCE. **SERVES 6 TO 8**

75 g (2¾ oz) stoned dates, chopped

2 pieces preserved stem ginger, finely chopped

1 ripe banana, mashed

2 tbsp ginger syrup (from the bottle of stem ginger)

125 g (4½ oz) margarine or butter

100 g (3½ oz) light muscavado sugar

2 large eggs, beaten

250 g (9 oz) wholewheat flour

1½ tsp baking powder

Pinch of salt

2 tbsp milk

1 Preheat the oven to 190°C/375°F/Gas 5, then lightly grease and line a deep 18-cm (7-in) cake tin.

2 Mix together the dates, ginger, banana and ginger syrup. Cream the margarine and sugar together until pale and creamy, then beat in the eggs a little at a time. Mix together the flour, baking powder and salt, and fold into the egg mixture. Fold in the date and banana mix, then add a little milk to give a soft, dropping consistency.

3 Turn into the prepared tin and smooth the top. Bake in the preheated oven for 30 to 35 minutes, until a toothpick inserted into the centre comes out clean, and the pudding shrinks away from the sides of the tin. Serve cut into wedges with cream.

warm spiced compote

THE MORE TYPES OF FRUIT, THE TASTIER THE DISH. **SERVES 6**

250 g (9 oz) chopped dried mixed fruits
225 ml (8 fl oz) water
350 ml (12 fl oz) orange juice
½ tsp cardamom seeds
1 cinnamon stick, broken

Thick plain yoghurt
50 g (1¾ oz) chopped brazil nuts

1 Place the fruits in a small pan with the water and orange juice. Crush the cardamom seeds lightly and add them to the fruit with the cinnamon stick. Heat gently until almost boiling, then remove the pan from the heat, cover and leave to stand for 3 to 4 hours.

2 Remove the cinnamon stick and reheat the fruit gently before serving, topped with yoghurt and chopped brazil nuts.

carrot pudding

A GREAT DESSERT TO FOLLOW A CURRY OR SPICY DISH. **SERVES 3 TO 4**

350 ml (12 fl oz) milk

½ tsp cardamom seeds

1 cinnamon stick, broken

6 cloves

125 g (4½ oz) grated carrot

25 g (1 oz) shelled unsalted pistachios

40 g (1½ oz) stoned dates, chopped

1 tsp light muscavado sugar

3 large eggs, beaten

1 Heat the milk with the spices until almost boiling, then remove from the heat and leave to stand 20 minutes before straining. Preheat the oven to 160°C/325°F/Gas 3.

2 Mix the carrot, pistachios and dates and transfer to a lightly greased pie dish. Beat the sugar with the eggs, then add the strained milk. Pour the mixture over the carrots, stir briefly and bake in the preheated oven for about 1½ hours, or until set. Serve warm with a sweet biscuit, such as shortbread.

sweet fruit pilau

A CREAMY RICE PUDDING ENHANCED BY TROPICAL FRUITS. **SERVES 4**

50 g (1¾ oz) pudding rice

1 tbsp light muscavado sugar

6 cloves

2 bay leaves

425 ml (¾ pt) milk

225 ml (8 fl oz) single cream

1 small orange

1 large ripe mango, chopped

100 g (3½ oz) seedless grapes, halved

1 Preheat the oven to 150°C/300°F/Gas 2. Place the rice in a large ovenproof dish with the sugar and spices, then add the milk and cream. Stir briefly and bake in the preheated oven for 2 hours. The rice will be creamier and wetter than for a traditional rice pudding.

2 Remove the skin and bay leaves from the pudding; leave for 20 minutes to cool. Meanwhile, prepare the fruit. Grate the rind from the orange and reserve it for decoration, then peel the fruit and chop the flesh roughly. Mix the orange with the mango and grapes, then stir the fruit into the warm rice. Serve immediately.

sweet bean and apple crumble

ADZUKI BEANS ARE SLIGHTLY SWEET AND MAKE A DELICIOUS DESSERT BASE. **SERVES 6**

50 g (1¾ oz) adzuki beans, soaked overnight, or tinned

½ tsp ground cinnamon

50 g (1¾ oz) honey

225 g (8 oz) finely sliced baking apples

CRUMBLE

75 g (2¾ oz) butter

175 g (6 oz) wholewheat flour

40 g (1½ oz) All-Bran® cereal

1 tbsp light muscavado sugar

1 Drain the adzuki beans, then rinse them under cold running water. Bring to the boil in a pot of fresh water, cover and simmer for 30 minutes or until tender. Drain and set to one side.

2 Preheat the oven to 190°C/375°C/Gas 5. Combine the cinnamon and honey and mix into the apples and adzuki beans in a suitable ovenproof dish. Blend the butter into the flour, All-Bran® and sugar, then spoon the crumble mixture over the fruit. Bake in the preheated oven for 30 to 35 minutes, until the crumble has browned and set. Serve with custard, cream or yoghurt.

fresh apricots with dried cherries and ginger

CHERRIES AND GINGER DRAW OUT THE FLAVOUR OF THE APRICOTS. **SERVES 4**

8 large ripe apricots

50 g (1¾ oz) semi-dried cherries, chopped

4 pieces preserved stem ginger, finely chopped

4 tbsp ginger syrup (from the bottle of stem ginger)

1 Cut the apricots in half and remove the stones – cut the fruit into quarters if they are very large. Add the cherries, the ginger and the syrup from the ginger to the apricots.

2 Stir the fruit gently to coat it all in ginger syrup. Chill for no more than 45 minutes before serving.

banana and rhubarb trifle

TOSS THE BANANA SLICES IN LIME JUICE TO PREVENT THEM FROM BROWNING. **SERVES 6**

400–450 g (14–16 oz) cooked rhubarb pieces, fresh or tinned

3 large bananas, sliced

125 ml (4 fl oz) rhubarb juice or syrup, from the cooking process or the tin

Grated rind and juice of 1 lime

2 pieces preserved stem ginger, finely chopped

50 g (1¾ oz) honey

225 g (8 oz) thick plain yoghurt

15 g (½ oz) wheat germ

1 Purée the rhubarb, banana, rhubarb juice, lime rind and juice in a blender or food processor. Turn into a bowl and add the ginger with honey to taste.

2 Fold the yoghurt into the mixture with the wheat germ, then cover and chill for 1 to 2 hours. Serve decorated with a little extra wheat germ or lime zest.

strawberries with melon and orange

MELONS ARE MOSTLY WATER, BUT MIXED WITH BERRIES THEY MAKE A GREAT FIBRE-RICH DESSERT. **SERVES 4**

450 g (1 lb) halved fresh strawberries

1 small honeydew or cantaloupe melon, balled

2 small oranges

60 ml (2 fl oz) orange juice (optional)

Fresh mint leaves

1 Place the halved strawberries in a bowl with the melon balls. Peel the oranges and break into segments, then cut them in half or chop them roughly, depending on size. Add the oranges to the other fruit with any juices, adding extra orange juice if necessary. The fruit will usually create their own juice, especially if the melon is ripe.

2 Leave to stand for 30 minutes. Serve the fruit salad at room temperature, decorated with the fresh mint leaves.

pineapple with apricots and berries

AN UNUSUAL COMBINATION OF FRESH AND DRIED FRUITS. **SERVES 4**

100 g (3½ oz) dried apricots, soaked if necessary

1 large ripe pineapple

100 g (3½ oz) raspberries

100 g (3½ oz) blueberries

Sugar or honey to taste

Sprig of fresh mint, to garnish

1 Chop the apricots roughly. Cut the pineapple in half lengthwise if you wish to use it for serving, and cut away the flesh to leave a firm shell. Alternatively, peel the pineapple, core it and dice the flesh into large chunks.

2 Mix the prepared pineapple with the apricots, raspberries and blueberries, adding sugar as necessary, or drizzle with honey, then arrange the fruit in the prepared shell or on a serving dish. Chill lightly and garnish with mint before serving.

fig and pecan pie

FIGS ADD AN EXTRA TEXTURE, WITHOUT MAKING THE PIE TOO SWEET. **SERVES 8**

PASTRY

100 g (3½ oz) butter

225 g (8 oz) wholewheat flour

Pinch of salt

Warm water

FILLING

100 g (3½ oz) unsalted butter

50 g (1¾ oz) light muscavado sugar

150 ml (5½ fl oz) honey

2 tsp vanilla extract

1 tbsp coffee extract or extra-strong espresso coffee, cooled

50 ml (2 fl oz) whisky or orange juice

200 g (7 oz) fresh figs, chopped

200 g (7 oz) pecan halves

1 Preheat the oven to 190°C/375°F/Gas 5. Prepare the pastry by blending the butter into the flour and salt. Add sufficient warm water to make a firm dough, then roll out and use to line a 25-cm (10-in), loose-bottomed flan tin. Chill in the refrigerator while preparing the filling.

2 Cream the butter and sugar together until pale and creamy, then beat in the honey and vanilla. Add the coffee flavouring and the whisky; beat in the figs and half the pecans, chopped. The mixture will appear to curdle, but don't worry!

3 Place the pastry case on a baking tray, then spread the pastry with the filling. Arrange the remaining pecans on top of the pie. Bake in the preheated oven for 40 minutes. The filling will bubble up through the nuts during cooking, giving them a crunchy coating. Serve the pie warm or cold, with ice cream or yoghurt.

pineapple oat meringues

THESE MERINGUES ARE NOT TOO SWEET AND HAVE A WONDERFUL COMBINATION OF FLAVOURS. **SERVES 4**

2 tbsp oats

4 slices fresh pineapple, cored

75 g (2¾ oz) raisins

2 large egg whites

100 g (3½ oz) caster sugar

1 Preheat the oven to 190°C/375°F/Gas 5. Toast the oats until golden brown, either in a hot dry frying pan or under a preheated grill. Leave to cool.

2 Arrange the pineapple slices in individual ovenproof dishes and fill the centres with raisins. Whisk the egg whites to stiff peaks, then gradually whisk in the sugar. Fold in the toasted oatmeal, then spoon the mixture over the pineapple in the dishes, covering the fruit completely.

3 Bake in the preheated oven for 5 to 8 minutes, until set and lightly browned. Serve immediately.

mincemeat and apple tart

THE APPLES IN THE TART ADD LIGHTNESS TO THE RICH MINCEMEAT. **SERVES 6**

PASTRY

75 g (2¾ oz) butter

175 g (6 oz) wholewheat flour

Grated rind and juice of 1 orange

**1 to 2 red-skinned dessert apples,
   cored and sliced**

350 g (12 oz) mincemeat

Juice of 1 lemon

2 tbsp honey

1 Preheat the oven to 190°C/375°F/Gas 5. Blend the butter into the flour, then stir in the orange rind. Bind the pastry with the orange juice, then roll it out and line a 20-cm (8-in) cake or flan tin. Toss the apples with the lemon juice.

2 Spread the mincemeat evenly in the pastry tin and arrange the sliced apples around the edge. Bake the tart in the preheated oven for 30 to 35 minutes.

3 Brush the apples carefully with honey as soon as the tart is removed from the oven, then leave to cool slightly before serving.

summer fruit upside-down trifle

USE FLAVOURED YOGHURT, IF YOU PREFER. **SERVES 6 TO 8**

900 g (2 lb) berries, fresh or frozen

175 g (6 oz) light muscavado sugar

50 g (1¾ oz) butter

225 g (8 oz) crushed digestive biscuits

75 g (2¾ oz) whole almonds, finely chopped

225 ml (8 fl oz) plain yoghurt

1 Cook the berries with the sugar over low heat until they just start to burst. Strain off 100 ml (3½ fluid ounces) syrup and set aside to cool. Melt the butter, stir in the biscuit crumbs and almonds and mix well. Set aside. Mix the cooled syrup with the yoghurt.

2 Place the berries in the bottom of a glass serving dish; top with the flavoured yoghurt. Make a thick layer of the crumbs over the trifle, then chill for at least 30 minutes before serving.

spiced berry pudding

A FRESH FRUITY ALTERNATIVE TO HEAVY WINTER PUDDINGS. **SERVES 8**

700 g (1½ lb) mixed berries, fresh or frozen

125 g (4½ oz) light muscavado sugar

1 tsp ground cinnamon

1 small fruit loaf, unsliced

1 Cook the berries with the sugar and cinnamon until they start to burst, then remove from the heat and set to one side.

2 Remove the crusts from the bread and cut it into 5-mm (¼-in) slices. Arrange the slices in a suitable pudding mould, cutting them so that they fit the mould neatly. Remove the bread and dip it, on both sides, in the fruit juices, then return it to the mould. Add the berries, removing them from the pan with a slotted spoon. Add sufficient juice to almost cover the berries (the bread will absorb a little more juice), then cover the pudding with more bread, dipping the slices into the juices.

3 Cover the pudding with a plate or saucer that will just sit on top of the bread, and place some heavy weights or tins on the plate. Allow the pudding to cool, then chill it for at least 6 hours or overnight.

4 To serve, carefully turn the pudding out onto a serving plate; if it has been well weighted and properly chilled, it should turn out easily and keep its shape. Serve with any remaining juices and yoghurt or cream.

tangerine and cream cheese pancakes

OTHER FRUITS SUCH AS PEARS AND PEACHES ALSO WORK VERY WELL. **MAKES 8, SERVES 4**

FILLING

100 g (3½ oz) low-fat cream cheese

1 tbsp light muscavado sugar

125 ml (4 fl oz) soured cream

4 tangerines or clementines, broken into segments

BATTER

1 large egg

300 ml (½ pt) milk

175 g (6 oz) wholewheat flour

Sunflower oil

1 Beat the cream cheese with the sugar, then blend in the soured cream. Set the filling to one side. Cut the tangerine segments in half if they are very big.

2 Preheat the oven to 190°C/375°F/Gas 5. Blend the egg and milk in a blender or food processor, then add the flour with the motor running. Blend to a smooth batter.

3 Heat a non-stick frying pan until hot, then brush the bottom lightly with oil. Pour a little of the batter into the pan and cook quickly for about 1½ minutes, then turn or flip the pancake over and cook the second side. Stack the cooked pancakes, interleaved in kitchen paper or greaseproof paper, until all the batter is used.

4 Divide the cream cheese mixture among the pancakes, spreading it evenly, then top with the tangerine segments. Roll up the pancakes, or fold them into quarters, and arrange in a large, ovenproof dish. Bake for 10 to 15 minutes in the preheated oven, just until heated through. Serve immediately while still hot.

prune and brandy mousse

A PRUNE PURÉE COMBINED WITH CREAM AND EGG WHITES TO MAKE A LIGHT MOUSSE. THIS RECIPE CONTAINS UNCOOKED EGG WHITE. **SERVES 6**

225 g (8 oz) stoned prunes

125 ml (4 fl oz) brandy, or orange juice and brandy mixed

1 to 2 tbsp light muscavado sugar

225 ml (8 fl oz) whipping cream

225 ml (8 fl oz) single cream

2 large egg whites

1 Purée the prunes with the brandy in a blender or food processor until smooth, then sweeten to taste.

2 Whip the creams together until soft and floppy – do not beat until stiff – then fold the cream into the prune purée. Whisk the egg whites until stiff; fold them into the prune cream. Turn into a serving bowl or 6 individual glasses and chill lightly before serving.

atholl brose

THIS TRADITIONAL SCOTTISH DISH OF OATMEAL, CREAM AND HONEY IS UTTERLY ADDICTIVE. **SERVES 6 TO 8**

50 g (1¾ oz) oatmeal

350 ml (12 fl oz) whipping cream

225 ml (8 fl oz) single cream

2 to 3 tbsp honey

50 ml (2 fl oz) whisky

Grated rind and juice of 1 medium orange

225 g (8 oz) raspberries

1 Toast the oatmeal until golden brown, either in a hot, dry frying pan or under a preheated grill. Allow to cool.

2 Whisk the creams together until thick and floppy but not stiff. Add the honey, whisky and orange juice and whisk briefly until they are evenly incorporated into the cream. Fold in the oatmeal, orange rind and raspberries, then turn into a serving bowl and chill lightly. Decorate with orange zest and mint before serving.

orange and sultana rice pudding

USE ONLY THE ORANGE RIND; JUICE WILL CURDLE THE PUDDING. **SERVES 3 TO 4**

50 g (1¾ oz) pudding rice

50 g (1¾ oz) sultanas

1 tsp light muscavado sugar

Grated rind of 1 medium orange

425 ml (¾ pt) milk

1 to 2 tbsp margarine or butter

Nutmeg, freshly grated

1 Preheat the oven to 150°C/300°F/Gas 2. Place the rice and sultanas in a lightly buttered casserole, and add the sugar and orange rind. Pour in the milk and stir to combine. Dot the top of the pudding with slivers of margarine or butter and sprinkle with nutmeg.

2 Bake the pudding slowly in the preheated oven for 2 hours. Serve hot or cold.

fig baked apples

DESPITE THEIR RELATIVELY LONG COOKING TIME, BAKED APPLES ARE AN EASY, DELICIOUS WINTER DESSERT; JUST PUT IN THE OVEN TO COOK WHILE YOU EAT YOUR DINNER. **SERVES 4**

4 medium cooking apples

100 g (3½ oz) dried figs, chopped

1 tbsp sultanas

3 tbsp honey

Yoghurt, custard or cream to serve

1 Preheat the oven to 175°C/350°F/Gas 4. Carefully remove the apple cores, either with a corer or a small, sharp knife. Pierce the skin of each apple to prevent it from bursting during cooking, then place in a buttered ovenproof dish.

2 Mix the chopped figs with the sultanas, then pack into the apples. Drizzle the honey over the apples, then pour half a cup of water into the bottom of the dish. Bake the apples in the preheated oven for about 45 minutes, until just tender – test them with the tip of a sharp knife. Do not overcook, or the apples will collapse. Serve hot with yoghurt, custard or cream.

danish apple cake

SERVE TOPPED WITH WHIPPED CREAM AND DUSTED WITH CHOCOLATE. **SERVES 4 TO 6**

175 g (6 oz) fresh wholewheat breadcrumbs

50 g (1¾ oz) Demerara sugar

75 g (2¾ oz) butter

450 g (1 lb) cooking apples, peeled, cored and sliced

Grated rind and juice of 1 lemon

1 Mix the breadcrumbs with the sugar. Melt the butter in a large frying pan, add the crumb mixture and fry quickly until the crumbs are crisp, then set them to one side.

2 Cook the apples with the lemon rind and juice and as little water as possible, until soft. I usually cook apples in a microwave because no water is required. Allow to cool.

3 Turn half the apples into a glass dish, then make a layer of half the crumbs over the apples. Repeat the layers, finishing with the remaining crumbs. Allow the pudding to cool completely, then chill for at least 1 hour before serving.

soft fruits with lime mascarpone

SWEET FRUITS SERVED WITH A RICH AND WICKED LIME-
FLAVOURED CREAM MIXED WITH TOASTED NUTS. **SERVES 4**

50 g (1¾ oz) hazelnuts or almonds

4 ripe peaches

1 tbsp lemon juice

250 g (9 oz) raspberries

250 g (9 oz) mascarpone cheese or crème fraîche

2 tbsp thick plain yoghurt

Grated rind and juice of 1 lime

1 tbsp caster sugar

Lime juice, to serve

1 Toast the nuts until golden brown in a non-stick frying pan or under a grill, then leave to cool before chopping finely.

2 Cut the peaches in half and remove the stones, then toss the peaches quickly in the lemon juice to prevent discolouration. Arrange the peaches on individual plates with the fresh raspberries.

3 Beat the mascarpone until smooth, then add the yoghurt, lime rind and juice, and beat again. Add sugar to taste and fold in the chopped nuts. Serve with the prepared fruits, drizzled with lime juice.

5 Breads, cakes and biscuits

High-fibre baking is quite different from baking with refined white flour. Bran tends to absorb liquid and, as the wholewheat kernel with all the bran is ground for wholewheat flour, I find it necessary to add more liquid than I would with white flour. I notice it especially with cakes and quick breads.

Different flours always have different characteristics and liquid absorption rates, so even if you always use the same brand, be prepared to check a mixture and adjust the liquid if necessary. This particularly applies to bread making. It is easy to add more, but taking away is difficult, so always add the measured amount gradually. I like to bake with stone-ground or organic flours, both of which produce silky doughs. Again, the water absorption rate of these flours tends to be different from regular wholewheat flour.

You may be able to find "fine" wholewheat flour in your area. If so, use it for pastry, cakes and cookies, sauces and batters. It is often labelled "for cakes and pastry" on the bag and has revolutionized high-fibre baking, producing lighter results. There is little point in sieving any wholewheat flour, as you will simply remove the bran from it.

These baking recipes have all been selected for their fibre content, but that does not mean that they are suitable for eating all day long! The cakes and biscuits are still high in calories and should be eaten as a treat rather than as a basic part of your diet. Homemade wholewheat bread is far more filling than commercial bread, so you should require less of it.

LEFT HONEYED GINGER CAKE (SEE PAGE 208)

toasted hazelnut rye bread

THIS IS AN EXCELLENT LOAF, FULL OF NUTTY TASTE AND TEXTURE. **MAKES 1 LARGE LOAF**

450 g (1 lb) wholewheat flour

250 g (9 oz) rye flour

2 tsp salt

40 g (1½ oz) poppy seeds

50 g (1¾ oz) toasted hazelnuts, chopped

1 sachet easy-blend yeast

3 tbsp hazelnut or olive oil

425 ml (¾ pt) warm water

1 Mix the flours, salt, poppy seeds, nuts and yeast together in a large bowl. Add the oil and sufficient water to form a manageable dough. Turn onto a lightly floured surface and knead thoroughly for about 5 minutes, until the dough is smooth – it will not become as elastic as a pure wheat dough. Shape into a round loaf and place on a lightly oiled baking tray, then cover and leave in a warm place for about 1 hour, until the dough has almost doubled in size.

2 Preheat the oven to 220°C/425°F/Gas 7. Score the top of the loaf with a sharp knife, if wished, then bake for 40 minutes until the base of the loaf sounds hollow when tapped. Cool on a wire rack.

barley and rye bread

BARLEY FLOUR IS SLIGHTLY SWEET AND COMBINES WELL WITH THE MORE SOUR FLAVOUR OF THE RYE.
MAKES 1 LOAF

350 ml (12 fl oz) warm water

350 g (12 oz) wholewheat flour

2 packets active dry yeast

125 g (4½ oz) barley flour

125 g (4½ oz) rye flour

1 Place the water in a large bowl; add 175 g (6 ounces) wholewheat flour and one packet of yeast. Blend to a smooth paste, then cover and leave in a warm place for 30 minutes, until full of bubbles.

2 Add the barley and rye flours to the ferment along with the salt and the remaining yeast. Gradually add the remaining wholewheat flour, using as much as necessary to produce a workable dough. Turn out onto a lightly floured surface and knead thoroughly for about 10 minutes, until smooth. This dough will not become elastic.

3 Shape into a loaf and place in a large, greased loaf tin. Cover and leave in a warm place for about 1 hour, until well risen.

4 Preheat oven to 220°C/425°F/Gas 7. Sprinkle flour over the loaf and bake for 35 to 40 minutes, until it sounds hollow when tapped. Turn out and cool on a wire rack.

pumpkin and cheese bread

THE PUMPKIN PURÉE ADDS MOISTURE TO THE LOAF. **MAKES 1 LOAF**

325 g (11½ oz) wholewheat bread flour

1 tsp salt

1 packet active dry yeast

1 tbsp olive oil

225 g (8 oz) thick pumpkin purée

225 ml (8 fl oz) warm water

75 g (2¾ oz) grated Cheddar cheese

1 Place the flour and salt in a large bowl and stir in the yeast. Make a well in the centre and add the oil and pumpkin purée, then mix to a manageable dough with the water. Turn onto a lightly floured surface and knead thoroughly for about 10 minutes until elastic. Return the dough to the bowl, cover and leave in a warm place for about 1 hour, until doubled in size.

2 Punch down the dough, kneading it lightly to incorporate the grated cheese. Shape into a round and place on a lightly greased baking tray, then cover the dough and leave for a further 40 minutes until well risen.

3 Preheat the oven to 220°C/425°F/Gas 7. Sprinkle a little wholewheat flour over the loaf, then bake for 35 to 40 minutes. Cool on a wire rack.

pear and banana bread

OTHER FRUITS CAN BE USED, BUT THIS IS MY FAVOURITE
COMBINATION. **MAKES 1 LARGE LOAF**

500 g (1 lb 2 oz) wholewheat flour
40 g (1½ oz) bran
1½ tsp bicarbonate of soda
1 tsp baking powder
Pinch of salt
40 g (1½ oz) light muscavado sugar
80 g (3 oz) dried pears, chopped
2 medium bananas, mashed
1 large egg, beaten
425 ml (¾ pt) buttermilk

1 Preheat the oven to 175°C/350°F/Gas 4 and lightly grease a
large loaf tin.

2 Place all the dry ingredients in a bowl and mix together,
adding the chopped pears. Make a well in the centre and add
the banana. Beat the egg into the buttermilk, pour it over the
banana and mix together briefly – this is like a soda bread and
should not be overworked, or it will not rise.

3 Spoon the mixture into the prepared tin, then bake in the
preheated oven for 1 hour, or until a toothpick inserted into the
loaf comes out clean. Cool in the pan for a few minutes, then turn
out onto a wire rack to cool completely.

spiced orange breakfast bread

THIS LOAF, BASED ON SWEDISH LIMPA BREAD, IS SPICED AND FLAVOURED WITH ORANGE AND MAKES A
WONDERFUL BREAKFAST BREAD. **MAKES 1 LOAF**

225 ml (8 fl oz) water

1 tsp caraway seeds

1 tbsp fennel seeds

1 tbsp clear honey

Grated rind of 1 orange

225 g (8 oz) rye flour

**350 g (12 oz) wholewheat
    bread flour**

1 tsp salt

1 packet active dry yeast

2 tbsp olive oil

1 Heat the water with the spices, honey and orange rind
until the honey has dissolved and the mixture is hot but
not boiling. Leave to cool until tepid.

2 Mix all the dry ingredients together in a large bowl and
add the oil. Pour the spiced water into the flours and mix
to a manageable dough, adding the juice from the orange if
the mixture is too dry. Knead thoroughly until the dough is
smooth – this combination of flours will not produce a soft
and really stretchy dough. Return the dough to the bowl,
cover and leave in a warm place for 1 hour, until well risen.

3 Punch the dough down, kneading it lightly, then shape
into a loaf and place in a greased loaf tin. Cover and leave
for a further 40 minutes.

4 Preheat oven to 220°C/425°F/Gas 7. Bake loaf for
45 minutes, remove from the tin and cool on a rack.

light rye sourdough

THE WHOLEWHEAT FLOUR ADDS GLUTEN TO THE RYE FLOUR, MAKING A LIGHTER BREAD. **MAKES 1 LOAF**

425 ml (¾ pt) tepid milk

600 g (1¼ lbs) wholewheat bread flour

2 packets active dry yeast

325 g (11½ oz) rye flour

1 tbsp salt

1 Place the milk in a large bowl, then stir in 350 g (12 ounces) of wholewheat bread flour and one packet of yeast. Blend until smooth, cover and leave in a warm place for 14 hours – this is best done overnight.

2 Mix the rye flour, salt and remaining yeast into the mixture and add as much of the wholewheat bread flour as necessary to give a manageable dough. Turn onto a lightly floured surface and knead thoroughly until smooth – the dough will not become very elastic.

3 Shape into a round loaf and place on a floured baking tray, or shape and place in a greased loaf tin. Cover and leave in a warm place for about 1 hour, until well risen.

4 Preheat the oven to 220°C/425°F/Gas 7. Bake the loaf for 20 minutes, then reduce the temperature to 190°C/375°F/Gas 5 and continue cooking for a further 20 minutes. Turn the loaf out onto a wire rack to cool.

wheaty soda bread

THE SECRET OF A LIGHT SODA BREAD LOAF IS TO NOT OVERMIX. THE DOUGH SHOULD JUST BE GATHERED TOGETHER AND NEVER KNEADED. **MAKES 1 LOAF**

500 g (1 lb 2 oz) wholewheat flour

40 g (1½ oz) bran

Pinch of salt

2 tsp bicarbonate of soda

1 tbsp light muscavado sugar

425 ml (¾ pt) buttermilk

1 Preheat the oven to 200°C/400°F/Gas 6 and lightly grease a deep 18-cm (7-in) round cake tin.

2 Mix together all the dry ingredients, then add the buttermilk and mix quickly with a broad-bladed knife. Turn the dough out of the bowl and bring it together gently with your hands – do not actually knead the dough or overwork it, as this will make the bread heavy. Form into a round and place in the prepared cake tin.

3 Bake the soda bread in the preheated oven for 40 minutes, then turn out and cool on a wire rack. Eat the soda bread on the day it is baked.

potato griddle scones

WARM POTATO MAKES LIGHTER SCONES, SO HEAT THE POTATO THROUGH (A MICROWAVE WORKS WELL) BEFORE MIXING THE DOUGH. **MAKES ABOUT 20**

400 g (14 oz) mashed potato

½ tsp salt

1 tbsp margarine or butter

100 g (3½ oz) wholewheat flour

1 Mix the mashed potato with the salt and margarine, then add sufficient flour to produce a stiff dough. Knead lightly on a floured surface and roll out to a 0.5 cm (¼ in) thickness. Cut into 5-cm (2-in) rounds.

2 Preheat a griddle or heavy frying pan, then cook the scones for 4 to 5 minutes, until lightly browned on both sides, turning once. Serve spread with butter or margarine.

grant loaves

THESE ARE COMMONLY NAMED AFTER DORIS GRANT, A WHOLEFOOD CAMPAIGNER WHO PERFECTED A LOAF PREPARED WITH NO KNEADING. IT WORKS WELL DESPITE BREAKING BAKING CONVENTIONS! **MAKES 3 LOAVES**

1.35 kg (3 lb) stone-ground wholewheat flour

2 tsp salt

2 packets active dry yeast

150 g (5½ oz) chopped walnuts, pumpkin and sunflower seeds, mixed

2 tsp molasses

1.25 l (2 pts) warm water

1 Lightly grease three large loaf tins. Have the flour, mixing bowl and loaf tins warm, especially in cold weather – this is a quick loaf to mix and cook, but because of the yeast it does require warmth. You can warm them by placing the flour in the mixing bowl and place in a very low oven with the loaf tins for 20 minutes.

2 Place the flour, salt, yeast, nuts and seeds in a large, warm bowl and mix well. Add the molasses to the warm water and whisk until blended. Make a large well in the centre of the flour add the water. Mix with a wooden spoon, scraping the flour from the edge of the bowl. Continue mixing until a dough is formed, then mix with your hands until it leaves the sides of the bowl. The dough should be sticky but not wet. Preheat the oven to 200°C/400°F/Gas 6.

3 Turn onto a very lightly floured surface and divide into three – the dough will be much softer and stickier than a regular dough. Shape roughly and place in the loaf tins. Cover, and leave in a warm place for 30 to 40 minutes, until the dough has risen slightly. Bake the loaves in the hot oven for 35 to 40 minutes, until the bases sound hollow when tapped. Cool on a wire rack.

quick onion and nut loaf

THIS IS A GREAT LOAF TO SERVE WITH SOUPS AND CHOWDERS. **MAKES 1 LOAF**

350 g (12 oz) wholewheat flour

2 tsp baking powder

½ tsp salt

1 tbsp margarine or butter

2 tbsp chopped parsley

100 g (3½ oz) coarsely grated onion

50 g (1¾ oz) pecan nuts, chopped

1 large egg, beaten

1 tsp Dijon mustard

225 ml (8 fl oz) milk

1 Preheat the oven to 190°C/375°F/Gas 5 and lightly grease a small loaf tin.

2 Mix all the dry ingredients together in a bowl, then blend in the margarine. Stir in the parsley, onion and pecans. Beat the egg with the mustard and add to the milk. Pour the liquid into the flour and mix to a stiff, wet batter. Transfer the mixture into the prepared loaf tin – it will almost fill it – and smooth the top.

3 Bake in the preheated oven for 45 to 50 minutes, until set and lightly browned. Cool for a few minutes in the tin, then turn out onto a wire rack to cool.

wild rice quick bread

THIS MAKES A DELICIOUSLY MOIST LOAF THAT IS ESPECIALLY GOOD WITH GOAT'S CHEESE. **MAKES 1 LOAF**

75 g (2¾ oz) wild rice

600 ml (1 pt) water

2 tbsp molasses

2 tbsp olive oil

225 g (8 oz) wholewheat flour

2 tsp baking powder

½ tsp salt

2 tbsp chopped fresh chives

50 g (1¾ oz) walnut pieces, chopped

1 large egg, beaten

1 Bring the rice to the boil in the water, then cover the pan and cook for 45 minutes, until the rice has nearly absorbed the water and the grains have split. Stir the molasses into the rice, and leave to cool for 30 minutes.

2 Preheat the oven to 160°C/325°F/Gas 3 and lightly grease a large loaf tin. Add the oil to the rice, then beat in the flour, baking powder, salt, chives and walnuts. Beat the egg into the mixture and then pour it into the prepared loaf tin. Smooth the top and bake for 1 hour, or until a toothpick inserted into the loaf comes out clean.

3 Loosen the loaf in the tin, then turn it out carefully onto a wire rack to cool. Serve with soft goat's cheese, if you like.

malted grain bread

A GREAT BREAD FOR BEGINNERS, THE METHOD ENCOURAGES YOU TO KEEP ADDING FLOUR UNTIL YOU HAVE THE CORRECT TEXTURE. **MAKES 2 LARGE LOAVES**

750 ml (1½ pts) tepid water

1.2 kg (2 lb 12 oz) malted grain flour

2 packets active dry yeast

1 tbsp salt

50 ml (2 fl oz) olive oil (optional)

1 Place the water in a large bowl – use the mixer bowl if you intend to knead the dough by machine. Sprinkle 400 g (14 ounces) flour on the water with the yeast, then mix to a smooth creamy paste. Cover and leave in a warm place for about 30 minutes, until very frothy.

2 Add the salt and oil to the yeast, then work in the remaining flour until the dough is easily manageable and does not stick to the work surface. Knead thoroughly until smooth and fairly elastic, then halve the dough and shape into loaves. Place the loaves on floured baking trays or in lightly greased loaf tins. The dough should fill the loaf tins just over half. Cover and leave in a warm place for about 40 minutes, until almost doubled in size. Preheat the oven to 220°C/425°F/ Gas 7. Sprinkle a little extra flour over the loaves, then bake in the preheated oven for 45 minutes, or until the base sounds hollow when tapped. Cool on a wire rack.

bran bread

THE ALL-BRAN® CEREAL ADDS BRAN TO THE RECIPE BUT GIVES IT A LIGHT, APPEALING COLOUR.

MAKES 1 LOAF

450 g (1 lb) wholewheat bread flour

1 tsp salt

40 g (1½ oz) All-Bran® cereal

1 packet easy-blend dried yeast

2 tbsp oil

**350 ml (12 fl oz) warm milk and
water, mixed**

1 Place the flour, salt and All-Bran® in a bowl; stir in the yeast. Add the oil, then add sufficient of the milk and water mixture to give a soft, manageable dough. You may find that you need a little extra liquid – the All-Bran® will absorb quite a lot.

2 Turn onto a floured surface and knead thoroughly for about 10 minutes until smooth. Shape into a round loaf and place on a lightly greased baking tray. Cover and leave in a warm place for about 1 hour, until well risen.

3 Preheat the oven to 220°C/425°F/Gas 7. Press a little extra All-Bran® lightly into the top of the loaf, then bake for 30 to 35 minutes. The base of the loaf should sound hollow when tapped. Transfer to a wire rack to cool.

wholewheat cheese rolls

I LIKE TO ADD A LITTLE WHITE FLOUR TO THIS MIXTURE, WHICH SHOULD BE SOFT AND SILKY. **MAKES 8**

50 g (1¾ oz) lard, margarine or butter

450 g (1 lb) wholewheat bread flour

175 g (6 oz) plain flour

1 tsp salt

1 packet active dry yeast

225 ml (8 fl oz) warm milk and water, mixed

40 g (1½ oz) sunflower seeds

40 g (1½ oz) grated Cheddar cheese

1 Blend the lard into the flours and salt in a large bowl. Stir in the yeast and mix to a manageable dough with the warm liquid, adding a little extra if necessary. Knead thoroughly on a lightly floured surface until soft and elastic, return the dough to the bowl, cover and leave in a warm place for about 1½ hours, until doubled in size.

2 Punch the dough down, kneading it lightly to incorporate the sunflower seeds. Shape into eight rolls, then roll out until 1.25 cm (½ in) thick. Place the rolls on lightly greased baking trays, cover and leave in a warm place for a further 30 to 40 minutes.

3 Preheat the oven to 200°C/400°F/Gas 6. Sprinkle the cheese over the rolls and bake in the preheated oven for 15 to 20 minutes. Transfer to a wire rack to cool.

chapatis

DO NOT OVERCOOK THESE INDIAN FLATBREADS OR THEY WILL BECOME HARD. **MAKES 6**

1 tbsp butter

175 g (6 oz) wholewheat flour

Good pinch of salt

About 75 ml (2½ fl oz) warm water

1 Blend the butter into the flour and salt, then mix to a soft dough with the water – add the liquid gradually, as the amount required depends on the flour being used. Turn onto a floured surface and knead until smooth and pliable. Return the dough to the bowl, cover and leave in a warm place for 30 minutes.

2 Divide the dough into six balls. Dip in a little extra flour, then roll them out into circles approximately 15 cm (6 in) in diameter.

3 Heat a griddle or a non-stick frying pan until evenly hot, and cook the chapatis for about 30 seconds on each side – turn them when brown spots start to appear on the surface. Keep the cooked breads warm in a clean teatowel until all the chapatis are cooked. Serve warm.

creamed corn cornbread

A SWEET, YET SAVOURY, BREAD, THIS MAKES A GOOD LUNCHTIME
SNACK OR CAN BE USED IN PLACE OF POTATOES, RICE OR PASTA WITH
A MEAL. **MAKES 1 LARGE LOAF**

100 g (3½ oz) yellow cornmeal

175 g (6 oz) wholewheat flour

2½ tsp baking powder

1 tbsp light muscavado sugar

2 tbsp dried pepper flakes or
   1 tbsp dried chilli flakes (optional)

½ tsp salt

3 large eggs, separated

425-g (15-oz) tin creamed corn

150 ml (¼ pt) whipping cream

125 g (4½ oz) butter, melted

1 Preheat the oven to 190°C/375°F/Gas 5 and lightly grease a deep
20- or 23-cm (8- or 9-in) round cake tin.

2 Mix all the dry ingredients together in a large bowl. Separate
the eggs and combine the yolks with the remaining
ingredients. Whisk the egg whites until stiff. Beat the corn mixture
into the dry ingredients until well mixed, then fold the egg white
through the mixture until evenly blended. Pour into the prepared
cake tin and bake in the preheated oven for 45 minutes, until
lightly browned and set.

3 Carefully remove the cornbread from the tin and allow it to
cool slightly before serving warm. It may also be served hot,
straight from the oven, as part of a meal.

molasses cornbread

I PREFER THIS RECIPE TO A CORNBREAD MADE WITH BAKING POWDER. **MAKES 1 LOAF**

75 g (2¾ oz) molasses

50 ml (2 fl oz) olive oil

300 ml (½ pt) milk

425 g (15 oz) wholewheat flour

250 g (9 oz) cornmeal

2 tsp salt

2 packets active dry yeast

1 Heat the molasses, oil and milk together until the molasses has blended with the other ingredients. Remove from the heat and allow to cool. Mix the flour, cornmeal, salt and yeast together in a large bowl and make a well in the centre. Pour in the cooled molasses mixture and mix to a manageable dough.

2 Knead thoroughly until smooth – this dough will not become elastic. Shape into a loaf and place in a large, greased loaf tin, then cover and leave in a warm place for 1½ hours, until risen just above the top of the loaf tin.

3 Preheat the oven to 220°C/425°F/Gas 7 while the dough is rising. Sprinkle a little extra cornmeal over the loaf and bake for 35 minutes, or until the base of the loaf sounds hollow when tapped. Cool on a wire rack.

wholewheat sandwich loaf

THIS IS A GREAT EVERYDAY BREAD THAT CHILDREN WILL LOVE. **MAKES 2 LARGE LOAVES**

1 kg (2¼ lbs) wholewheat bread flour

225 g (8 oz) white bread flour

1 tbsp salt

2 packets active dry yeast

50 ml (2 fl oz) olive oil

750 ml (1½ pts) tepid water

1 Place all the dry ingredients in a large bowl and mix in the yeast. Add the oil and most of the water, then mix to a workable dough, adding the remaining water if necessary. Turn out onto a floured surface and knead thoroughly for about 10 minutes until smooth and fairly elastic.

2 Shape the dough into two loaves. Place the loaves either on floured baking trays or in lightly greased loaf tins. The dough should fill the loaf tins just over half. Cover and leave in a warm place for about 40 minutes, until well-risen and almost doubled in size.

3 Preheat the oven to 220°C/425°F/Gas 7. Sprinkle a little extra flour over the loaves, then bake in the preheated oven for 45 minutes, or until the bases sound hollow when tapped. Cool on a wire rack.

wholewheat morning rolls

THIS OVERNIGHT DOUGH MAKES CREAMY, SOFT ROLLS FOR BREAKFAST. **MAKES 18**

OVERNIGHT

600 ml (1 pt) warm water

500 g (18 oz) wholewheat bread flour

1 tbsp salt

1 packet active dry yeast

MORNING

1 packet active dry yeast

175 ml (6 fl oz) warm water

600 g (1¼ lbs) wholewheat bread flour

75 g (2¾ oz) margarine or butter

1 tsp light muscavado sugar

1 Place the water for the overnight dough in a large bowl. Add the flour, salt and yeast and mix lightly – do not beat or knead. Cover and leave overnight at room temperature.

2 In the morning, add all the remaining ingredients to the bowl and mix to a manageable dough; the margarine will be incorporated during the mixing. Turn out onto a floured surface and knead well for about 10 minutes until the dough has become smooth and elastic.

3 Shape the dough into 18 rolls. Place them on lightly greased baking trays, just touching. Cover and leave in a warm place for 30 minutes to rise.

4 Preheat the oven to 220°C/425°F/Gas 7. Bake the rolls for about 20 minutes. The bases will sound hollow when tapped, but the tops of the rolls will only brown slightly and remain soft. Cool on a wire rack.

sultana scones

A DELICIOUS TREAT FOR AFTERNOON TEA! **MAKES 12**

2 tbsp butter

400 g (14 oz) wholewheat flour

2 tsp baking powder

40 g (1½ oz) light muscavado sugar

75 g (2¾ oz) sultanas

1 large egg, beaten

About 150 ml (¼ pt) milk

1 Preheat the oven to 220°C/425°F/Gas 7 and lightly grease a large baking tray. Blend the butter into the flour and baking powder, then stir in the sugar and sultanas. Make a well in the centre and pour in the beaten egg. Mix to a soft dough with the milk.

2 Knead the dough on a lightly floured surface until smooth, then roll out until 1.25-cm (½-in) thick. Cut out with a 5-cm (2-in) cutter and place the scones on the prepared baking tray.

3 Bake for 10 minutes in the preheated oven, then cool slightly on a wire rack before serving.

cheese and walnut scone rounds

THESE SCONES ARE A PERFECT ACCOMPANIMENT TO SOUPS AND STEWS. **SERVES 4 TO 8**

100 g (3½ oz) butter

350 g (12 oz) wholewheat flour

2 tsp baking powder

Pinch of salt

50 g (1¾ oz) walnuts, chopped

100 g (3½ oz) grated Cheddar cheese

1 large egg, beaten

8 tbsp milk

1 Preheat the oven to 220°C/425°F/Gas 7 and lightly oil a baking tray.

2 Blend the butter into the flour, baking powder and salt, and stir in the nuts and cheese. Beat the egg with the milk and use to mix to a soft but manageable dough.

3 Turn onto a lightly floured surface then knead lightly until smooth. Shape the dough into a round about 2.5 cm (1 in) thick, and score eight portions. Bake on the baking tray for 20 to 25 minutes. Cool for at least 10 minutes.

wholewheat drop scones

ALSO KNOWN AS SCOTCH PANCAKES, THESE ARE QUICK TO MAKE AND DELICIOUS TO EAT. **MAKES ABOUT 12**

125 g (4½ oz) wholewheat flour

1 tsp baking powder

Pinch of salt

1 large egg, beaten

150 ml (¼ pt) milk, or milk and water mixed

1 Mix the flour, baking powder and salt together in a bowl and make a well in the centre. Beat the egg with the milk, add it to the flour and beat to a smooth, thick batter.

2 Heat a heavy frying pan until evenly hot, then drop tablespoonfuls of the mixture onto the surface, allowing room for them to spread slightly. Turn the scones after a minute or so, when bubbles begin to rise to the surface. Cook for a further 1 to 2 minutes, then serve.

sticky buns

EVEN WHEN MADE THE HIGH-FIBRE WAY, THESE YEASTED BUNS ARE
UTTERLY DECADENT AND TOTALLY DELICIOUS. **MAKES 8**

350 g (12 oz) wholewheat bread flour

1 packet active dry yeast

150 ml (¼ pt) warm milk

1 tbsp margarine or butter

½ tsp salt

1 egg, beaten

FILLING

50 g (1¾ oz) butter or margarine

40 g (1½ oz) light muscavado sugar

2 tsp mixed spice

100 g (3½ oz) currants or raisins

1 Place 40 g (1½ ounces) flour in a small bowl with the yeast and add the warm milk. Mix to a smooth paste, cover and leave in a warm place for 25 to 30 minutes until frothy. Blend the margarine into the remaining flour and salt in a large bowl; make a well in the centre. Beat the egg and pour it into the dry ingredients. Add the yeast and mix into a manageable dough. Knead thoroughly until smooth and elastic, then return the dough to the bowl. Cover and leave in a warm place for about 1½ hours, until doubled in size.

2 Lightly grease a deep 20-cm (8-in), round baking tin. Melt together the butter, sugar and spice for the filling and allow to cool slightly. Pour half the mixture into the tin and spread evenly over the base. Punch the dough down by kneading lightly, then roll out into a rectangle about 30 x 20 cm (12 x 8 in). Spread the remaining syrup over the dough, then sprinkle with the currants. Roll up, trim the ends, then cut the dough into eight pieces. Place them in the tin with the joins towards the centre. Cover and leave in a warm place for a further 40 minutes.

3 Preheat the oven to 190°C/375°F/Gas 5. Bake the buns in the preheated oven for about 25 minutes. Leave in the tin to cool for 2 to 3 minutes before turning out onto a wire rack to cool.

rock buns

125 g (4½ oz) butter or margarine

350 g (12 oz) wholewheat flour

1 heaped tsp baking powder

Pinch of salt

1 to 2 tsp mixed spice

175 g (6 oz) dried mixed fruit, such as sultanas, currants, cranberries

1 egg, beaten

100 ml (3½ fl oz) milk

1 Preheat the oven to 200°C/400°F/Gas 6 and lightly grease some muffin tins. Blend the butter into the flour, baking powder, salt and spice in a bowl until the mixture resembles fine breadcrumbs. Stir in the fruit, add the beaten egg and the milk, and mix to a stiff dough.

2 Place spoonfuls of mixture in the prepared muffin tins and bake in the preheated oven for 20 to 25 minutes. Cool on a wire rack.

wholewheat honey and pecan bread

THIS IS A QUICK-MIX YEASTED LOAF, BEST SERVED SLICED AND BUTTERED, WITH JAM OR HONEY.

500 g (18 oz) wholewheat bread flour

75 g (2¾ oz) wheat germ

½ tsp salt

1 packet active dry yeast

100 g (3½ oz) raisins

100 g (3½ oz) toasted hazelnuts, chopped

2 tbsp sunflower oil

50 ml (1¾ fl oz) honey

225–300 ml (8–10 fl oz) warm water

1 Mix all the dry ingredients together in a large bowl and make a well in the centre. Add the oil, honey and 225 ml (8 fluid ounces) warm water, then mix to form a manageable dough, adding extra water as necessary. Do not add too much water or the dough will become very sticky.

2 Turn the dough out onto a lightly floured surface and knead thoroughly until smooth. Shape into a loaf and place in a large, greased loaf tin – the dough should fill to just over half. Cover and leave in a warm place for about 1 hour, until well risen.

3 Preheat the oven to 220°C/425°F/Gas 7. Bake the loaf for 10 minutes, then reduce the temperature to 200°C/400°F/Gas 6 and continue cooking for a further 30 to 35 minutes. Cool on a wire rack, then serve sliced and buttered.

quick bran teabread

THE MIXTURE IS VERY WET WHEN IT GOES INTO THE OVEN AND IS USUALLY FROTHING. DON'T WORRY – THIS IS HOW IT SHOULD BE. **MAKES 1 LOAF**

150 g (6 oz) mixed dried fruit

225 ml (8 fl oz) cold tea

75 g (2¾ oz) light muscavado sugar

50 g (1¾ oz) margarine

3 tbsp orange marmalade

150 g (6 oz) wholewheat flour

1 tsp baking powder

1 tsp bicarbonate of soda

1 tsp mixed spice

Pinch of salt

50 g (1¾ oz) All-Bran® cereal

1 egg, beaten

1 Preheat the oven to 175°C/350°F/Gas 4 and lightly grease a large loaf tin. Place the dried fruit, tea, sugar, margarine and marmalade in a saucepan and heat gently until the sugar has dissolved and the margarine melted, then leave to cool.

2 Mix the dry ingredients together in a large bowl and make a well in the centre. Beat the egg and add it to the fruit mixture, then pour into the dry ingredients and mix thoroughly and quickly. Pour immediately into the prepared loaf tin. Bake in the preheated oven for 50 to 60 minutes, until a toothpick inserted into the loaf comes out clean.

3 Cool the teabread on a wire rack. Serve sliced and lightly buttered.

banana cornmeal muffins

DELICIOUSLY LIGHT MUFFINS, WITH JUST A HINT OF GINGER. **MAKES 12**

175 g (6 oz) wholewheat flour

50 g (1¾ oz) cornmeal

75 g (2¾ oz) light muscavado sugar

1½ tsp baking powder

½ tsp bicarbonate of soda

Pinch of salt

1 tsp ground ginger

3 medium bananas, roughly mashed

2 large eggs, beaten

225 ml (8 fl oz) soured cream

1 tbsp margarine or butter, melted, or oil

1 Preheat the oven to 175°C/350°F/Gas 4 and line 12 muffin tins with paper cases.

2 Mix all the dry ingredients together in a bowl and add the bananas. Beat the eggs with the soured cream and add the melted margarine. Pour into the dry ingredients and work quickly until the mixture is combined together – do not beat.

3 Divide the mixture among the muffin tins, then bake in the preheated oven for 25 minutes, until a toothpick inserted into the muffins comes out clean. Cool briefly on a wire rack. Serve warm.

fig cake

THE ORANGE JUICE PREVENTS THE MIXTURE FROM BECOMING TOO SWEET. **MAKES 1 CAKE**

225 g (8 oz) roughly chopped dried figs

Grated rind and juice of 1 medium orange

175 g (6 oz) butter

350 g (12 oz) wholewheat flour

Pinch of salt

50 g (1¾ oz) soft brown sugar

1 large egg, beaten

1 Place the figs, orange rind and juice in a pan and cook slowly for 10 to 15 minutes until soft. Mash together gently with a wooden spoon, then set aside.

2 Blend the butter into the flour, salt and sugar. Add the egg and sufficient water to mix to a manageable dough. Roll out half the mixture and press into the bottom of a 20-cm (8-in) baking tin with a loose bottom, then spread with the figs. Roll the remaining dough into a circle just a little smaller than the tin, then place over the figs and press down firmly sealing the two crusts together. Chill the fig cake while preheating the oven.

3 Preheat the oven to 190°C/375°F/Gas 5. Bake the cake for 30 minutes, or until the dough is set. Mark into eight to ten segments while still warm, then cut when completely cold.

blueberry-pecan bran muffins

THE MIXTURE WILL BE SLIGHTLY WETTER THAN YOU EXPECT, BUT THE BRAN WILL ABSORB THE EXTRA MOISTURE. **MAKES 6**

50 g (1¾ oz) butter

1 large egg, beaten

125 ml (4 fl oz) milk

40 g (1½ oz) light muscavado sugar

125 g (4½ oz) wholewheat flour

15 g (½ oz) bran

1½ tsp baking powder

125 g (4½ oz) blueberries

40 g (1½ oz) pecans, finely chopped

1 Preheat the oven to 200°C/400°F/Gas 6 and double-line six large muffin tins with paper cases. Melt the butter and leave it to cool slightly. Beat the egg with the milk, add the sugar and leave to stand.

2 Mix all the dry ingredients together in a bowl and add the blueberries and chopped nuts. Mix the butter with the milk and egg, then pour into the bowl and mix quickly and lightly – this should take no more than a few seconds. Do not beat the mixture, which will seem rather wet.

3 Divide the mixture among the six prepared muffin tins and bake immediately in the preheated oven for 30 minutes. Cool briefly on a wire rack and serve warm.

courgette and raisin cake

A MOIST VERSION OF THE CONVENTIONAL CARROT CAKE. **MAKES 1 LARGE CAKE**

275 g (9¾ oz) wholewheat flour

1 tsp bicarbonate of soda

2 tsp baking powder

1 tsp ground ginger

175 g (6 oz) light muscavado sugar

100 g (3½ oz) raisins or sultanas

175 g (6 oz) grated courgette,
   closely packed

150 g (5½ oz) grated carrot

150 g (5½ oz) plain yoghurt

3 large eggs, beaten

150 ml (¼ pt) corn oil

1 Preheat the oven to 175°C/350°F/Gas 4, and line a 23-cm (9-in) round cake tin with baking parchment.

2 Place the flour, bicarbonate of soda, baking powder, ginger, sugar and raisins in a bowl, then mix in the courgette and carrot. Add the yoghurt with the eggs, then finally add the oil. Mix to a thick batter and beat vigorously for 1 minute. Pour the mixture into the prepared tin, and bake in the preheated oven for 1 hour, until a toothpick inserted into the mixture comes out clean. Cool slightly, then turn out onto a wire rack and leave to cool.

muesli cake

THIS IS BEST STORED FOR 2 TO 3 DAYS BEFORE EATING. **MAKES 1 CAKE**

175 g (6 oz) muesli

75 g (2¾ oz) light muscavado sugar

100 ml (3½ fl oz) clear honey

150 g (6 oz) sultanas

225 ml (8 fl oz) unsweetened grape
   or orange juice

175 g (6 oz) wholewheat flour

2 tsp baking powder

1 tsp bicarbonate of soda

2 tsp mixed spice

1 large egg, beaten

1 Preheat the oven to 160°C/325°F/Gas 3, then grease and line an 18 x 28-cm (7 x 11-in) cake tin. Heat the muesli, sugar, honey and raisins with the fruit juice until the sugar has dissolved; leave to cool for 10 minutes.

2 Mix together the dry ingredients. Add the beaten egg to the muesli mix, then add the dry ingredients and quickly beat into a thick, frothy paste. Pour into the prepared cake tin, lightly smooth the top and bake in the preheated oven for 40 minutes. Cool slightly, then mark into squares. Allow to cool completely on a wire rack before cutting to store in an airtight container.

honeyed ginger cake

THE HONEY MAKES THIS MILDER THAN MOST GINGER CAKES.

MAKES 1 LOAF CAKE

100 g (3½ oz) margarine or butter

100 ml (3½ fl oz) honey

75 g (2¾ oz) light muscavado sugar

350 g (12 oz) wholewheat flour

1½ tsp bicarbonate of soda

2 tsp ground ginger

2 large eggs, beaten

2 tbsp milk

1 Preheat the oven to 160°C/325°F/Gas 3 and line a 28 x 18-cm (11 x 7-in) tin with baking parchment.

2 Heat the margarine, honey and sugar together over low heat until the margarine has melted and the sugar dissolved – do not allow the mixture to boil or the cake will become crusty. Remove from the heat and leave to cool.

3 Mix the dry ingredients together in a large bowl and make a well in the centre. Beat the eggs with the milk and stir into the honey mixture. Add to the dry ingredients and mix thoroughly. Pour into the prepared tin and bake in the preheated oven for 40 minutes, or until a toothpick inserted into the cake comes out clean. Remove from the tin and cool completely on a wire rack. Wrap in foil or store in an airtight container for 1 to 2 days to allow the flavour to develop before eating. Drizzle with icing, if you like.

date squares

THIS CAKE IS DELICIOUS BUT IS HIGH IN CALORIES, SO IS BEST FOR OCCASIONAL TREATS. **SERVES 8 TO 10**

250 g (9 oz) dates, chopped

150 ml (¼ pt) water

1 tsp vanilla essence

175 g (6 oz) butter

150 g (5½ oz) rolled oats

175 g (6 oz) wholewheat flour

150 g (5½ oz) light muscavado sugar

1 Preheat the oven to 175°C/350°F/Gas 4 and line a deep 20-cm (8-in) sandwich tin. Place the dates and water in a saucepan and cook slowly until the dates are soft, the water is slightly reduced and the mixture can be beaten into a thick purée. Add the vanilla and set the mixture aside.

2 Melt the butter in a saucepan, then stir in the remaining ingredients. Press half the mixture into the bottom of the prepared tin, then top it with the date mixture and then the remaining oat mixture. Smooth the top, then bake in the preheated oven for 30 minutes.

3 Mark into portions while still warm, then leave to cool completely before slicing. Store in an airtight container.

pineapple raisin cake

AN EVERYDAY FRUIT CAKE, EMBELLISHED WITH UNUSUAL DRIED FRUIT. **MAKES 1 MEDIUM CAKE**

150 g (5½ oz) dried mixed fruit (pineapple, sultanas, dried cranberries, and so on)

125 ml (4 fl oz) pineapple or orange juice

175 g (6 oz) margarine or butter

350 g (12 oz) wholewheat flour

2 tsp baking powder

Pinch of salt

1 tsp ground ginger

75 g (2¾ oz) light muscavado sugar

2 large eggs, beaten

1 Soak the fruit in the fruit juice for 10 minutes. Preheat the oven to 175°C/350°F/Gas 4 and lightly grease a deep 18-cm (7-in) round cake tin.

2 Blend the butter into the flour, baking powder, salt and ginger in a bowl until the mixture resembles fine breadcrumbs. Stir in the sugar, then add the fruits and juice and the beaten eggs. Mix to smooth batter adding a little extra fruit juice or milk as required, then spoon the mixture into the prepared cake tin.

3 Bake in the preheated oven for 1¼ hours, or until the cake stops "singing" – yes, go on, listen to it – and a toothpick inserted into the centre comes out clean.

4 Cool slightly in the tin, then turn out carefully onto a wire rack to cool completely.

cranberry coffee cake

A LIGHT SPONGE CAKE TO SERVE PLAIN OR WITH CREAM AND FRESH FRUITS. **MAKES 1 CAKE**

3 large eggs

50 g (1¾ oz) light muscavado sugar

125 g (4½ oz) wholewheat flour

1 tbsp sunflower oil

1 tsp coffee flavouring or very strong cold espresso coffee

25 g (1 oz) dried cranberries, chopped

1 Preheat the oven to 190°C/375°F/Gas 5 then lightly grease a 20- to 23-cm (8- to 9-in) cake tin and line the base with baking parchment.

2 Whisk the eggs and sugar together until pale and fluffy – this is best done in an electric mixer and may take up to 10 minutes. Fold in the flour a few spoonfuls at a time, then add the oil and coffee, drizzling them down the side of the bowl. Finally, add the cranberries, folding in lightly. Transfer the mixture immediately to the prepared cake tin and bake in the preheated oven for 20 to 25 minutes, until the mixture springs back when pressed lightly and shrinks away from the sides of the tin.

3 Turn the cake out onto a wire rack to cool completely. Decorate with fruit and whipped cream, if wished, then serve sliced.

carrot cake

I AM VERY GENEROUS WITH THE FROSTING ON THIS WONDERFUL CAKE
– YOU CAN'T BE GOOD ALL THE TIME! **MAKES 1 LARGE CAKE**

350 g (12 oz) wholewheat flour

2 tsp baking powder

1 tsp bicarbonate of soda

1 tsp salt

1 tsp mixed spice (optional)

50 g (1¾ oz) walnut pieces, finely chopped

3 large eggs, beaten

2 bananas, mashed

50 g (5½ oz) grated carrot

175 ml (6 fl oz) sunflower oil

FROSTING

175 g (6 oz) softened unsalted butter

200 g (7 oz) cream cheese

1 tsp vanilla essence

300 g (10½ oz) icing sugar, sifted

1 Preheat the oven to 175°C/350°F/Gas 4 then lightly grease a deep 23-cm (9-in) round cake tin and line it with baking parchment.

2 Mix all the dry ingredients together in a large bowl, then add the eggs, mashed bananas and carrots. Pour the oil into the bowl and beat thoroughly to a thick, well-blended batter. Spoon into the prepared cake tin and bake in the centre of the preheated oven for about 1 hour, until a toothpick inserted into the cake comes out clean. Remove the cake carefully from the cake tin and allow to cool completely on a wire rack.

3 Prepare the frosting by beating together the softened butter and cream cheese until blended into the frosting, then add the vanilla essence and beat again. Sift the icing sugar and beat it gradually into the cheese mixture. Spread the frosting over the cooled cake and decorate, if wished, with finely chopped walnuts or a little extra grated carrot. Serve in thin slices.

213

rhubarb streusel cake

THE TOPPING GIVES A DELICIOUS CRUNCH IN CONTRAST TO THE MOIST RHUBARB. **MAKES 1 LARGE CAKE**

STREUSEL TOPPING

75 g (2¾ oz) butter

150 g (5½ oz) wholewheat flour

½ tsp baking powder

100 g (3½ oz) Demerara sugar

125 g (4½ oz) butter or margarine

100 g (3½ oz) light muscavado sugar

2 large eggs, beaten

175 g (6 oz) wholewheat flour

1 tsp baking powder

½ tsp cinnamon

1 tbsp milk

350 g (12 oz) rhubarb pieces, in 5-cm (2-in) lengths, fresh or tinned

1 Preheat oven to 175°C/350°F/Gas 4, line a deep 20-cm (8-in) round cake tin with baking parchment.

2 First prepare the topping. Blend the butter into the flour, baking powder and sugar until evenly distributed, then set aside. Cream the butter and sugar together until pale and fluffy, then gradually add the beaten eggs. Mix the flour, baking powder and cinnamon together and fold it into the mixture, adding the milk to make a smooth batter.

3 Spoon the cake mixture into the prepared tin. Arrange the rhubarb over the cake and cover with the topping mixture, spreading it evenly.

4 Bake the cake in the preheated oven for 1 hour, or until a toothpick inserted into the cake comes out clean. Leave in the tin for 2 to 3 minutes, then remove the cake carefully, peel off the paper, and allow to cool completely on a wire rack.

parkin

SIMILAR TO GINGERBREAD IN TASTE, WITH A ROUGHER TEXTURE. DON'T LET THE MOLASSES BOIL OR YOU WILL GET A TOUGH CRUST. **MAKES 1 CAKE**

225 g (8 oz) black treacle or molasses

40 g (1½ oz) light muscavado sugar

125 g (4½ oz) margarine or butter

225 g (8 oz) wholewheat flour

2 tsp baking powder

Pinch of salt

150 g (6 oz) pin head or Irish oatmeal

2 large eggs, beaten

About 150 ml (¼ pt) milk to mix

1 Preheat the oven to 160°C/325°F/Gas 3 and line a 28 x 18-cm (11 x 7-in) tin with baking parchment.

2 Heat the molasses, sugar and margarine gently until the margarine has melted and the sugar has dissolved. Leave to cool slightly. Mix all the dry ingredients together in a large bowl and make a well in the centre. Add the beaten eggs to the liquid and pour into the dry ingredients; mix thoroughly, adding sufficient milk to give a soft, runny consistency.

3 Pour the batter quickly into the prepared tin and bake in the preheated oven for 1 hour. Carefully transfer onto a wire rack to cool. Cut into squares when cold and store in an airtight container until required.

wholewheat cinnamon biscuits

PERFECT FOR DUNKING IN COFFEE OR HOT CHOCOLATE. **MAKES 18**

50 g (1¾ oz) butter

100 g (3½ oz) wholewheat flour

½ tsp freshly grated nutmeg

100 g (3½ oz) light muscavado sugar

1 medium egg, beaten

2 tbsp Demerara sugar

1 tsp cinnamon

1 Blend the butter into the flour, nutmeg and brown sugar, then bind to a dough with the beaten egg. Turn out onto a floured surface and knead lightly until the dough is smooth. Cover in clingfilm and chill for at least 30 minutes.

2 Preheat the oven to 200°C/400°F/Gas 6. Shape into 18 walnut-sized pieces, then place on greased baking trays and flatten slightly with a fork. Mix together the Demerara sugar and cinnamon, and sprinkle the mixture over the biscuits. Bake for 12 to 15 minutes, swapping the trays halfway through cooking if necessary so they cook evenly. Cool on a wire rack and store in an airtight tin.

apricot muesli bars

THESE FRUIT MUESLI BARS MAKE FOR A SUBSTANTIAL SNACK OR EVEN A LIGHT MEAL SUBSTITUTE. **MAKES 8**

FILLING

200 g (7 oz) dried apricots, finely chopped
Grated rind and juice of 1 medium orange

75 g (2¾ oz) margarine or butter
100 ml (3½ fl oz) honey
225 g (8 oz) muesli
100 g (2¾ oz) wholewheat flour

1 Preheat the oven to 190°C/375°F/Gas 5 and lightly grease an 18-cm (7-in) square cake tin.

2 Cook the apricots with the orange rind and juice, simmering slowly until all the orange juice has disappeared. Allow to cool. Melt the margarine in a saucepan, add the honey and heat gently until melted into the margarine. Stir in the muesli and flour and mix well.

3 Press half the muesli mixture into the prepared cake tin, then cover with a layer of apricots. Top with the remaining muesli mixture, pressing it down and smoothing the top with a metal spoon. Try to poke any raisins into the mixture so that they do not burn.

4 Bake in the preheated oven for 20 to 25 minutes, until lightly browned. Mark into bars and allow to cool in the tin. Cut through, then cool completely on a wire rack. Store in an airtight container.

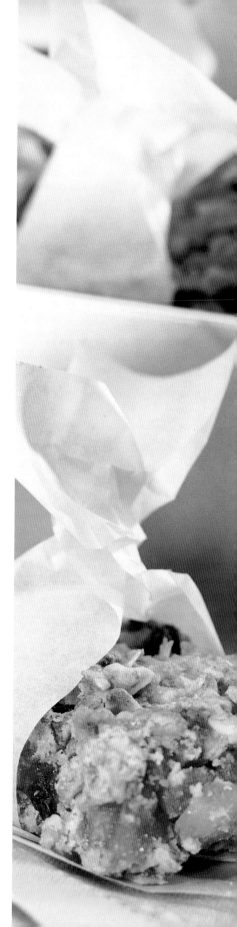

ABOVE PEANUT BUTTER BISCUITS

muesli biscuits

CHILL THE MIXTURE BEFORE BAKING OR THE BISCUITS WILL SPREAD TOO MUCH IN
THE OVEN. **MAKES ABOUT 20**

100 g (3½ oz) butter or margarine

75 g (2¾ oz) light muscavado sugar

75 ml (2¾ fl oz) honey

225 g (8 oz) low-fat muesli

100 g (3½ oz) wholewheat flour

1 Cream the butter and sugar together until pale and fluffy, then add the honey and beat thoroughly again. Work in the muesli and flour to give a stiff dough that is only slightly sticky, then turn out onto a lightly floured surface and knead firmly until the dough is easily manageable. Form into a sausage shape, about 30 cm (12 in) long, then cover in clingfilm and chill in the refrigerator for at least 30 minutes.

2 Preheat the oven to 175°C/350°F/Gas 4 and lightly grease two baking trays. Cut the biscuit dough into 20 pieces, form into balls, then flatten slightly and place on the prepared baking trays. Bake in the preheated oven for 12 to 15 minutes, until lightly browned. Leave the biscuits to cool slightly on the baking trays until firm enough to transfer to a wire rack to cool completely. Store in an airtight container or biscuit jar.

peanut butter biscuits

BEWARE, THESE BISCUITS ARE RICH! **MAKES 18**

100 g (3½ oz) crunchy peanut butter

50 g (1¾ oz) margarine

100 g (3½ oz) Demerara sugar

1 large egg, beaten

175 g (6 oz) wholewheat flour

1 tsp baking powder

1 Cream together the peanut butter, margarine and sugar, then add the beaten egg. Fold in the flour and baking powder and form into a stiff dough. Turn out onto a floured surface and knead lightly. Cover in clingfilm and chill for about 1½ hours, until firmer and easier to handle.

2 Preheat the oven to 175°C/350°F/Gas 4 and lightly grease two baking trays. Cut the dough into 18 slices and form each into a ball, then press lightly to flatten as you place them on the prepared baking trays. Dip a fork into a little flour and press it into the tops of the biscuits, then bake in the preheated oven for 15 to 20 minutes. Cool slightly before transferring to a wire rack to cool completely.

all-butter shortbread

BUTTER IS ESSENTIAL TO GIVE THIS BISCUIT THE MOST DELICIOUS FLAVOUR. **MAKES 1 LARGE SHORTBREAD**

100 g (3½ oz) slightly softened unsalted butter

175 g (6 oz) wholewheat flour, fine if available

Pinch of salt

50 g (1¾ oz) light muscavado sugar

1 Preheat the oven to 175°C/350°F/Gas 4 and lightly grease an 18-cm (7-in) baking tin – I usually line the tin with baking parchment, although this is not essential.

2 Blend the butter into the flour, salt and sugar in a bowl until the mixture resembles fine breadcrumbs. Turn into the prepared tin and press down with a broad-bladed knife. Lightly mark the shortbread into eight portions, then prick through to the base using a fork and make a decorative edge.

3 Bake in the preheated oven for 25 to 30 minutes. Cool slightly in the tin, then mark the shortbread into portions again before turning out onto a wire rack to cool. Cut through or break into portions when completely cooled.

walnut biscuits

IF YOU PREFER, COAT THE BISCUITS IN MELTED CHOCOLATE ONCE THEY HAVE COOLED. **MAKES ABOUT 30**

100 g (3½ oz) unsalted butter, slightly softened

100 g (3½ oz) light muscavado sugar

1 large egg, beaten

175 g (6 oz) wholewheat flour

1 tsp baking powder

75 g (2¾ oz) walnut pieces, finely chopped

1 Cream the butter and sugar together until pale – the mixture will be slightly sticky. Add the egg and mix well, fold in the flour and baking powder, then finally work in the nuts.

2 Turn the mixture out onto a lightly floured surface and knead gently to bring the dough together. Roll into a sausage shape about 30 cm (12 in) long, wrap in clingfilm, and chill for at least 1 hour, until firm enough to handle.

3 Preheat the oven to 175°C/350°F/Gas 4 and lightly grease two or three baking trays. Cut the dough into thin slices and roll them into balls about the size of a walnut. Place on the prepared baking trays, flattening the biscuits slightly with the palm of your hand. Bake for 12 to 15 minutes, then allow to cool slightly on the baking tray before transferring to a wire rack to cool completely.

Index